THE BLUE MOON DAY

Five Men's Magical Discovery Enroute Life

SANTHOSH SIVARAJ

First edition published in India in 2017

Second edition in 2018

ISBN: 978-93-87328-76-1

Invincible Publishers

G-120, Sushant Lok III, Sector 57, Gurgaon-122002

Registered Address: Opposite Kasturba Ashram, Radaur, Haryana - 135133

Printed at Thomson Press (India) LTD

Dedicated to my Big Fat Happy Family

Just as writing fast is a talent, Reading slowly is also a virtue. I would recommend that you read this book slowly, to gain the most from the experience.

Contents

PREFACE

It was 3:30 AM in the Pacific when I got ready for my 4:00 AM duty at the ship. I started my rounds from the open deck, inspecting the machinery spaces. On top of the deck, I noticed abnormal coloured smoke emanating from the funnel. I ignored the warning, thinking it to be the regular boiler emission problem. Later, I entered the engine room and took over the charge from the third engineer. His red eyes with the slow cat walk confirmed his excessive indulgence of Vodka on duty. At this juncture, expecting machinery data from him would be like expecting expenditure data from your wife after her shopping. I wished him goodnight and got back to my duty, all alone, as the other motorman who was supposed to join me on duty was sick.

I maneuvered through the machinery spaces and checked the critical parameters. Everything was normal, except for the engine room temperature, which according to me was relatively high. I kept spying around for any indication which could confirm my judgement and that was when I noticed smoke near the turbo charger space. I panicked, and without even raising the alarm, I rushed to the spot for inspection. The Turbo Charger was blood red in colour with its insulation pack burnt. I don't know if it was the toxic gas or some crazy spirit within the ship which had gotten into me that I decided to fight this fire with the portable fire extinguisher placed nearby. I remember aiming the foam at the turbo charger and a huge gush of something white knocked me down, unconscious. I simply had no idea what happened to me after that.

I tried to open my eyes and that was when I realized that the whole engine room was filled with smoke. The white smoke was too thick for me to see my own hands. I was suffocating badly and was panicking like hell. I could not shout, I could not see, I could not breathe and I could not hear. All I could do was run and I did just that. Even now, I am surprised how I made it through those steep ladders and the heavy doors.

By the time I pushed myself out on the open deck, I was almost a dead man walking. I grabbed the railings on the deck, still suffocating with my closed eyes. I composed myself and my breathing and opened my eyes to see a dream. There was this bright full moon, radiating its light on the calm blue sea with falling stars all across. Dolphins were diving gracefully making splashes on the otherwise static sea. I felt someone was trying to tell me something beautiful. It felt wonderful to be alive again.

It was my last journey as a sailor.

I was out on a no ball and therefore l got another chance to play. This time, with this bonus life, I decided to go only for sixers. This book is one of those sixers, inspired by real-life characters. I took the liberty of mixing them with my imagination. I hope you find yourself in one of these characters!

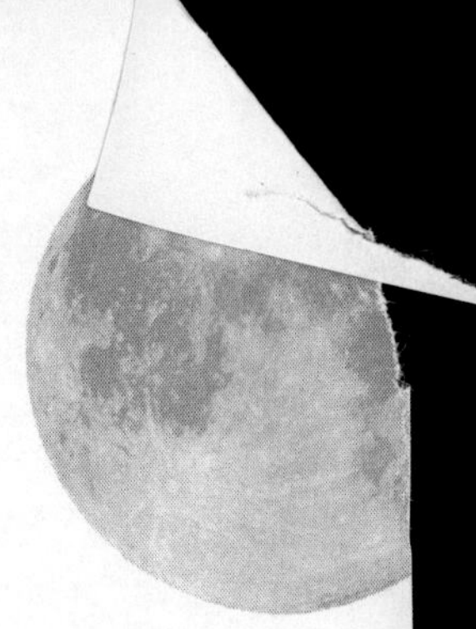

The Pizza Engineer

"I have to get through this!" Abi thought. "I have been a fighter all my life and I will fight this too. I topped every level of my education. Why can't I top this? I was the best outgoing student at college and my Ph.D. thesis won international accolades. All this makes me a winner! So, Abi, just make sure you present yourself in the best possible way and ensure that all your accomplishments are conveyed to the interview panel in a subtle yet powerful way!"

He continued to think. "So what if I am obese? It is only the obese and lazy ones who create ideas for easy and effective living. I am multitalented and have specialized qualifications in more than one way. My engineering degree is in the Mechanical field. My post-graduation is in the Management field and my doctorate is on Nano-technology. That makes me a versatile candidate. My clarity in communication and power to articulate thoughts are my strengths. I will make sure that my strengths are seen and my interests are discussed!"

Still waiting for his call, and left with nothing else to find in the empty waiting hall, he continued to think deeper. "Man, I should not waste anymore energy thinking! I must be fresh and ready to take this on with ease. Hope I've shaved properly! I have to do something with these nostril hairs. Sometimes, I look like a fat Charlie Chaplin. Anyway, if I get through this, I should start reorganizing myself and my finances. I am too lost nowadays. Looks like I have overloaded myself in all possible ways!"

"Mr. Abhinav!" called the lady in red. She had a fake smile plastered on her face while looking at Abhinav as if she was trying to say, "You are never too fat to get a job!"

Abi rose with a little struggle and tried to walk elegantly past the candidates. Just then, he realized that the front button of his shirt had popped out. Trying to avoid the attention, he walked across the room as if he had a minor wardrobe malfunction during a major catwalk.

❋❋❋

Abi entered the interview hall holding his file in front of his belly. He presented himself with the so-called interview attitude and sat with his arms crossed. He mentally rehearsed his well-prepared answer for the million dollar question: "Tell me about yourself."

Rishi, the white-bearded interviewer with an immersing smile, started the interview with his first question. "So, Mr. Abhinav, tell me five interesting weight loss tips!"

Abi's face became paler than the interviewer's beard.

Smiling like a little girl holding Barbie doll he replied, "Sir, actually I have started working out only recently. I am sure that results will start showing very soon!"

"Please don't take this personally, Abhinav!" Rishi interrupted. "I was just trying to break the ice! You know what? My wife is double my size and she comes up with a new diet every other month. The diet has been showing results, but only on me! She ends up adding extra pounds by eating those emotionally liberating snacks!"

Acknowledging the joke, Abi tried to smile tolerantly, without insulting his potential Boss' wife.

"So tell me Abhinav, what you do at the Gym?" Rishi continued with the topic.

Based on what he had seen in movies and advertisements, Abi said, "Sir, normally I spend maximum time on the treadmill and then do some pushups and stretches."

"That must be boring!" Rishi said. "I believe you should join a dance class or play a sport. In fact, you should do both and continue with the gym on alternate days. This can get you hooked to the habit of exercising without getting bored!"

"That's a good thought, sir!" Abi said. In his present condition, he wondered if he could fit into any activity other than belly dancing and sumo wrestling.

Reading Abi's resume, Rishi said, "Your educational background looks interesting, Abhinav! How come you chose different fields at every stage?"

"Sir, I had a great fascination towards machines and their operation which had pulled me to Mechanical Engineering. After my Engineering, I wanted to do my MBA to fit into the administrative side of a company. This can make me handle the operational and administrative part of any organization!" Abi said

"And what about the Ph.D.?" asked Rishi.

"Sir, in my MBA days, the principal had suggested that I pursue a Ph.D.. He offered a scholarship in his institution. I did not want to miss out on the opportunity!"

"But why Nano Drillers?" Rishi asked again.

"Sir, Nano Technology is a budding field and I wanted to grab the opportunity with both my hands," replied Abi with sincerity.

"Son, today the world has too many opportunities to hold onto, but unfortunately two hands are never enough. You better hold on to one thing tight before looking at others!" Rishi replied.

Abi acknowledged him with a serious nod as if he had heard the secret of attaining nirvana.

"Now let me get serious Abhinav, How do you think you fit into the role of a Research Analyst?" asked Rishi directly looking into Abi's eyes.

"Sir, you have seen my profile. I have a passion for research and it was something that kept me going during my MBA days. With Mathematics as my strength, I think I will do justice to this job!"

"Look, Abhinav. My experience says that you need this job badly, but to me, you are not qualified. We need an experienced hand for this job. You, according to me, are a fresher at 29. Your higher education indicates your lack of ability to land up in a job in your initial days and you have kept specializing, thereby narrowing your scope of opportunity. Your education in varied domains indicates your lack of vision or passion in one area. So tell me, how can I help you now?"

Abi was stunned. He wanted to say something, but he felt shallow inside. He just heard his deepest fear taking a sharp crisp voice. With a serious face, Abi tried to bring out all the courage left in him and said, "Sir, you have been seeing my resume only from a pessimistic point of view. I promise you that I have a lot to offer. Give me one chance, and I will promise you that it will be one of the best decisions you would have ever made!"

Acknowledging Abi's request, Rishi said, "Let me see son, if anything suitable comes up, I will definitely call you."

Accepting defeat, Abi rose up, forgetting to cover his open shirt. He thanked Rishi and left the room with an empty mind and a heavy heart. With the fourth consecutive failure for the month, Abi felt that all was lost for him. There was nothing that could console him and his sadness started to turn into fear. He sat on a park bench. He had all the possible qualifications with no job in sight. The comparisons he had with his friends did not matter now, as he was left way far behind. His age was catching up and there was no sense of accomplishment. He wanted to do something fast but for that he had to start somewhere. Nothing seemed to be in his vicinity and then his phone rang.

Seeing a new number, he didn't want to pick up. The phone rang again and this time he picked it up.

"Hello?" answered Abi in a muted voice.

"Is this Abhinav?" asked the caller.

"Yes," answered Abi with not much interest.

"You don't recognize the voice you heard in the morning?" asked the caller.

With a little thought, Abi realized that it was the voice of Rishi, the interviewer. "Oh, yes sir, I do!" he answered promptly.

"Listen, I am giving you another opportunity and this can land you in a bigger role than you can imagine. We have a vacancy in our Creative Division and we are looking for a person with special capacities. I somehow believe that you have it in you, but I don't know how. To get this job, you need to impress one man, Mr. Pillai – the founder of our company. So I just wanted to know if I can fix an appointment with him for you, if you are okay with it?"

"Sure sir, I am interested," Abi replied, without a pause.

"Okay, then, I shall mail you the time and venue of the appointment tonight and you better make the most out of it!"

"Sure sir!" said Abi, thanking Rishi repeatedly for his interest in him.

Just before hanging up, Rishi said "Abhinav, beware of Mr. Pillai. He is no ordinary guy and you better be prepared for anything and everything!"

❖❖❖

Abi was instructed to meet Mr. Pillai at 7:30 AM near the tower house. Abi could hardly sleep that night. He rehearsed a bunch of ways to interact with Mr. Pillai. Considering the early morning appointment, he was assuming it to be more of a casual interaction where Mr. Pillai would possibly be on for his morning walk or something. He was not sure what he should wear but was very sure of wearing a loose shirt with stronger buttons. With an average waking time of 10:00 AM, Abi made sure that he was not going to sleeping that night, thanks to 10 cups of coffee with an occasional snack.

Abi reached the venue at 6:30 AM and was amazed to see the place buzzing with activity. He started his countdown on teacups to support his drooping eyelids. The mail had informed him to stand beside the fruit shop near the tower house. It also informed him that Mr. Pillai would be in a white tee and a pair of blue trousers. Abi had already started his search for men dressed in a white tee and blue trousers. He assumed Mr. Pillai to be in his fifties and most probably a healthy and fit man.

The time was 7:30 AM, already, and Abi was getting anxious. He did not want to call Rishi as he believed it was still too early to disturb him. He started imagining things - what if Mr. Pillai had forgotten about the appointment? What if he expected Abi to find him? Continuing with his permutations and combinations, he gazed at an old man in a white tee and blue trousers playing with the local kids near the tower house. Abi thought he could be Mr. Pillai, but why would he be playing with local kids? He must have been this social man with a CSR outlook! He started walking towards this old man and stood at a distance of five feet from him.

The old man was teaching the kids how to plant saplings and was also carrying a dozen of small trees with him. The kids were too involved with this old man and were doing all that he was telling them.

Abi approached the old man and said, “Mr. Pillai?”

The old man looked back and gazed at Abi's face for a long time.

"Are you Mr. Pillai?" asked Abi with a gentle voice.

"Yes," came the immediate answer.

"Sir, I am Abhinav. I was instructed by your office to meet you at the beach house regarding the job at your company," said Abi in a clear tone.

"What Job?" the old man asked.

"Sir, I was informed about the vacancy in the creative department," said Abi.

"Oh yes, I remember now," said Mr. Pillai. "Before we get into any of that, you better help me with planting some saplings!"

"Sure sir," said Abi.

So in the early hours of the day amidst all the joggers and walkers, Abi was planting trees, dressed in his new formals and a little tie. Everyone was on their knees planting the trees when the sound of fabric tearing stopped them. It was Abi's pants. Realizing what had just happened, Abi immediately looked up and smiled at the kids like a cute version of Mr. Bean.

"Just un-tuck the shirt and continue with the work!" said Mr. Pillai, without even looking at Abi.

Imagining Mr. Pillai to be a hard task master, Abi continued working without any care for his torn pants. It was 8:30 AM when the job was done. Mr. Pillai bid his little friends goodbye, telling them the date and time for their next meet. He started a conversation with Abi while walking towards the road, with Abi catching up.

"Do you realize what I was trying to do with the kids?" asked Mr. Pillai.

"Yes sir, you were teaching them about plants, their specialty and how to plant them!" said Abi.

"That was just an excuse to be with them. I am a student when I am with them. Their questions amaze me as they are not constrained by any worldly theorems or by practical limitations. I become a kid with them and try to think the way they do!"

"Your outlook is interesting sir," said Abi with a sense of real involvement.

"And so are their questions!" said Mr. Pillai. "Today, one of the kids asked me, why the math tables have to be in complete digits like 1, 2, 3 and why not in decimals like 1.2, 2.3, 3.2 and so on."

"Oh really, did they? Today's kids are way ahead of us in a lot of aspects sir!" said Abi.

"Very true, Abi," conveyed Mr. Pillai. "To some extent, I think we are responsible for this. We have been raising the bar every day in terms of Knowledge and Technology. The future generations have no other option but to be smart. In other words, I would say that they are the slaves of our civilization."

"Well said, sir," Abi said.

"Tell me Abi, what do you think is the most powerful and special characteristic of a kid?" asked Mr. Pillai. Suspecting that his interview had already begun, Abi said, "Like you said before, their curiosity about things and their ability to ask questions, sir!"

"True, but I believe it is their power of imagination that makes them special. In fact, it is the need of the hour, not only for the kids but for adults too. Living in today's world requires a lot of imagination than we were expected to have!" said Mr. Pillai.

"Very true, Sir. I wonder why books for adults cease to have vivid characters and backgrounds like the books for kids!" said Abi.

"Hey, who stopped you from reading kids books?" asked Mr. Pillai.

Abi gave a soundless smile. Mr. Pillai continued, “I was speaking to one of my young friends the other day and was discussing the same topic with him. He said to me that his children were an inspiration for him. They helped him indirectly in coming up with imaginative ways to request for leave in his office or escape a fight with his wife!”

Abi continued to smile and said, “Now, I remember Sir. I am imaginative in finding excuses to wake up late everyday!” Realising what he had just said, Abi bit his tongue and said to himself, “Now stop digging your own grave a@!#$!”

“So Abi, tell me about yourself,” asked Mr. Pillai.

Abi took this well deserved chance to speak out all that he had rehearsed for the interview yesterday without any hiccups. Mr. Pillai listened keenly to every word Abi said, and was constantly smiling at him.

“Listen Abi, this position in our company is way too important for us as we believe it can change the company’s future for the good,” said Mr. Pillai.

“I understand it fully, Sir,” Abi replied in the most sincere way possible.

“So where do you live?” asked Mr. Pillai.

“Sir, I am put up at Besant Nagar near the shore.”

“Oh, that’s an excellent location!” exclaimed Mr. Pillai.

Utilizing the newfound closeness with Mr. Pillai, Abi asked, “Sir, what qualities do you expect from the person for this position?”

“Mmmm, too keen aren’t you?” asked Mr. Pillai, “This job involves more of the attitude than knowledge and therefore we have decided that the vacancy will not be filled in by an interview.”

“Then how...?” Abi asked. Forgetting to add ‘his trademark Sir’ at the end of the sentence.

"Well, I will stay with the job applicant for a couple of days and will analyze him over the stay," said Mr. Pillai.

"What the *hell*?" Abi thought. He started picturising his room with all the dirt, posters, and books and so on.

"What are you thinking about?" asked Mr. Pillai, studying Abi's silence.

"Nothing, Sir!" he replied in a jiffy.

"So when can I come?" asked Mr. Pillai.

"At your convenience, sir!" said Abi.

"Well, in that case, it is convenient right now," said Mr. Pillai to the mentally shocked Abi.

❋❋❋

Mr. Pillai sat on Abi's Bike and their journey started. Trying to accommodate Mr. Pillai on the bike in the best way possible, Abi literally sat on the tank while riding. As per Mr. Pillai's direction, Abi took the longest route to the destination which let them admire the beauty of the shore and enjoy the freshness of the breeze. As they entered the city, the traffic started. An old taxi with a right indicator stood in front of them. Understanding that the Taxi was about to take a right turn, Abi tried to overtake the taxi on the left side. Then, without any warning the taxi took a sharp left turn, hitting the bike and bringing both Abi and Mr. Pillai down. Realizing what had happened, the taxi driver stopped his vehicle and got out to help the duo.

"Are you mad?" shouted Abi with anger.

"Sorry sir, I didn't see your bike coming. Please forgive me sir!" begged the taxi driver. Trying not to create a scene in front of Mr. Pillai, Abi remained calm and checked if Mr. Pillai was okay. "Why did you take a left turn with the right indicator on," asked Mr. Pillai to the Taxi driver with keen interest.

"Sir, my left indicator is not working and I had to indicate someway that I was taking a turn and that's why I put the right indicator on!" said the taxi driver, sadly.

“That’s ridiculous!” exclaimed Abi.

“Leave it Abi, let’s move!” said Mr. Pillai in a casual voice. Sensing the relief in the taxi driver’s face, Abi said, “Don’t be stupid. Your mistake could have cost our lives!”

The driver accepted his mistake and had a long face till the duo got on their bike and continued their ride. It took another 20 minutes for them to reach the house. It was a compact apartment situated right at the beach site.

“Beautiful place!” exclaimed Mr. Pillai.

“This is one of the best shallow beaches you can find in this region, Sir,” said Abi.

“Oh really? You must be swimming in it every day then!” said Mr. Pillai.

“Not really, Sir, It was interesting initially but nowadays I hardly visit the beach.”

“Oh, come on, can anyone ever get bored of a beach?” exclaimed Mr. Pillai. After spending some time at the beach, they went up to Abi’s apartment.

“Sir, my apartment is in a bad condition. If I had any idea about your stay, I would have made it worthy of it!” said Abi sincerely.

“Oh, come on! It’s perfectly alright. I know how a bachelor’s house looks. I assumed you were living alone,” said Mr. Pillai.

“I live alone, yes, Sir,” replied Abi quickly without letting Mr. Pillai speak any more about this.

Reaching the entrance to Abi’s apartment, they noticed a dead sparrow on the floor.

“Not again!” exclaimed Abi. “This is the fourth dead sparrow in front of my apartment. It’s definitely somebody’s mischief!”

“Or maybe the Sparrows find solace dying in front of your apartment,” said Mr. Pillai with a friendly wink.

After clearing the sparrow's carcass, they entered the apartment. The apartment was worse than what Mr. Pillai had anticipated. It had clothes drying in the middle of the hall and papers strewn all around the floor. There were some interesting posters posted all around the house which were both educative and entertaining. The house looked squalid and it should have been ages since it was last cleaned. There were lots of books lying on the floor as well as stacked on the shelves. The kitchen looked comparatively cleaner, the less said about the bathrooms the better. Visually tired and disgusted by the smell, Mr. Pillai took the refuge in a comfortable chair in the balcony.

"Sir, give me 10 minutes, I will clean the house and make you comfortable!" said Abi trying to prevent Mr. Pillai from making a comment.

"Sure, go ahead!" said Mr. Pillai.

Abi tried to get hold of everything in his line of sight, and threw it into the store room. He told himself that this room was the savior for the day and should continue to remain the savior till Mr. Pillai left. After clearing the floor, he tore the posters off the wall. He tried to arrange the books in their shelves and the extra ones were thrown in the store room. He never tried to do anything about the smell, as he had gotten immune to it. He sprayed water all over the bathroom and assumed that it got cleaned.

"Please feel free, Sir!" said Abi.

"Oh, you need not worry about that. I have lived in a place worse than this!" said Mr. Pillai in a relaxed manner.

Not trying to judge whether the statement is a compliment or a comment, Abi continued his fast track cleaning spree. After dumping most of the stuff in the store room, the apartment looked a bit tolerable.

"So what is it that stops you from keeping your room tidy, Abi?" asked Mr. Pillai.

"Sorry sir. I have been on and off to my home town and I could not find time for maintenance," replied Abi.

"In that case can I assume your apartment was clean before that?" asked Mr. Pillai.

Avoiding excuses, Abi replied, "Sir, I am lazy when it comes to regular maintenance. I always try to keep things tidy but I keep postponing cleaning."

"I can see that," said Mr. Pillai, "Why do you keep thinking something or the other all the time?"

This came as a surprise to Abi. He had no answers to give and yet he said, "Sir, I believe it's a common thing with everybody."

"What if I say that it is the reason for your laziness?" asked Mr. Pillai.

"I don't get you, Sir," said Abi quite keenly.

"Your mind knows you better than anybody else does. It has conditioned you to do things in the most relaxed or a feel good way. It always tries to find the shortcut to do things or shortcut to avoid doing things. So until otherwise there is an emergency it tells you to just chill," said Mr. Pillai.

"You mean to say it is only my mind or is it the same for everybody?" asked Abi.

With a smile, Mr. Pillai replied "it is the same for everybody, however, some people condition their mind and in most cases the mind conditions the people."

Understanding what Mr. Pillai was trying to say, Abi asked, "How can one condition his mind, Sir?"

"Well, the first thing to condition or control your mind is to stop making it think!" Mr. Pillai said.

"Stop thinking?" asked Abi," Is that possible?"

"Sure, why not? In fact, it is a type of meditation!" said Mr. Pillai without a break.

"How can this help me, Sir?"

"Well, first of all, it can stop making you give excuse for not cleaning your apartment," said Mr. Pillai.

With a toothy smile, Abi asked, "I couldn't get you sir."

"Looks like I am the candidate here. I have to do all the answering!" Mr. Pillai remarked, "Man's mind has the potential to think innumerable things. But, unfortunately, he has gotten habituated to think little with time and that too the same thoughts repeatedly. And these thoughts are predominantly on fear and that too about the future which might or might not happen. In this process, he loses the absolute present. Little does he realize that this second now was his future a second ago. If he tries to stop all diversions and tries to keep a blank mind, he can succeed at anything in the present!"

"But this must need practice, right?" asked Abi.

"More than practice, it needs the will and reflexes," explained Mr. Pillai.

"How does this Zero thinking help me in keeping my room clean?" asked Abi.

"I will give you a suggestion. Everyday give yourself a Zero thinking hour and make sure you have a list of to do things which has been postponed by you for some time. In this Zero thinking hour start doing those things immediately without questioning it, without describing it and mainly without thinking about it!"

"That sounds possible," said Abi.

"Not that easy in the beginning. You will have all sorts of thoughts during that time but you persevere and practice this perseverance. You will finally succeed!"

Abi felt that he had gained something precious in this little discussion and promised himself to practice the Zero thinking hour every day. The discussion continued for some more time when Mr. Pillai decided to go to the beach and spend some time alone. Abi asked Mr. Pillai what he would prefer for lunch when he comes back.

"Anything!" replied Mr. Pillai with ease. "Another test, maybe!" thought Abi and started to plan the lunch menu within the limitations of the grocery and his expertise in the kitchen. He decided to make roti, tomato curry, rice with dal and yogurt to finish with. The war in the kitchen began and Abi Intentionally tried to practice Zero Thinking while cooking. Considering this a routine dish, he bought mushrooms and made chilly mushroom fry. He did not try to attempt egg recipes as he was not sure if Mr. Pillai would prefer it or not. After a couple of hours, Mr. Pillai entered Abi's house and was happy to smell something good this time.

"Smells great, hope it tastes great too!" said Mr. Pillai.

"I am not that good at cooking, Sir, but my prolonged bachelorhood has left me with no other choice but to cook!" said Abi in a funny tone.

"Yes, that's true because after losing your bachelorhood, you will become an expert in cooking in order to save your marriage," replied Mr. Pillai.

Trying not to start a joke again, Abi stopped conversing and started to serve the food. After tasting every item on the menu, Mr. Pillai said, "I don't think you are a beginner, you have a potential to get a black belt in cooking!"

"Thank you for the compliment, Sir! I realize now, why I am fat. It's my cooking skills!" said Abi, this time laughing at the joke himself. Mr. Pillai too joined in the laughter. After lunch, Abi suggested to Mr. Pillai to rest for some time, but Mr. Pillai had other plans. In the meantime, Abi could not control himself and slowly settled down on the couch in the hall.

Mr. Pillai had gone out again, this time to the nearby park for a little walk and returned around after a couple of hours.

Abi was still on the couch, but this time, he was sleeping way too comfortably on his tummy like a little baby.

After waiting for some time, Mr. Pillai couldn't stop himself from waking up Abi and told him to get ready for the evening walk. Abi thought If not for Mr. Pillai, he would have extended his nap to a REM sleep. He got ready in a jiffy with a quick face wash and lots of deodorant.

They walked towards the city and settled down at a lonely tea stall.

"So, Abi, what are your strengths and weaknesses?" asked Mr. Pillai.

Remembering his answers from the previous interviews, Abi said "Sir, I believe my strengths are my flexibility and versatility whereas I am a little lazy to begin with."

"I am convinced with your weakness part but can you explain your strengths?" asked Mr. Pillai.

"I believe I can do anything and everything, provided I am given time. I adjust to the situations and act according to the needs and the goals of the company."

"Forget the company, man. That's the last thing on my mind," said Mr. Pillai, "Can you launch a missile rocket tomorrow?"

"Sir, that sounds illogical, however, I believe I can do it if I am provided with all the essentials," answered Abi.

Acknowledging Abi's answer Mr. Pillai asked, "So you can do anything and everything. But, tell me, what is it that you want to do in life?"

Abi went quiet for a second and asked in a low voice, "You mean....?"

"Yes, I mean your passion," answered Mr. Pillai.

"That's a tough question to answer sir, as I believe I find passion in everything I do," said Abi.

"And what all do you do?" asked Mr. Pillai seriously.

"Well, all that a common individual does," answered Abi.

"Now stop boring me and tell me that you have not found your passion so far!" said Mr. Pillai in a strong voice.

Sensing the seriousness in Mr. Pillai's voice and finding no choice, he answered, "Yes sir, you are true but off late I am trying to identify it."

"And how will you do that?" asked Mr. Pillai.

This time Abi let Mr. Pillai give the answer, he said, "I am not sure, Sir."

"You have to try all the possible things at all possible times in all possible ways," he answered.

Not willing to say anything at the moment, Abi continued to gaze at Mr. Pillai's face indirectly signaling him that he needs more explanation.

Mr. Pillai asked, "Have you ever given a serious try at playing, acting, writing, teaching, public speaking, painting, web designing, fashion designing, cartooning, sculpting or any other thing different from your routine?"

"No sir, never tried anything like that!" answered Abi.

"Why?" asked Mr. Pillai.

"I didn't find time for it sir. I have been busy with academics all my life!"

"And was there anything you found there that you were passionate about?" asked Mr. Pillai again.

Abi remained silent, signifying a no.

"Education is a way to know things and passion comes from creating things, with or without knowledge. Study you before you study anything. You run with the masses, you will end up running all your life. Stop and introspect," detailed Mr. Pillai.

Mr. Pillai was gaining Abi's attention. Abi wanted to jump to Mr.Pillai's feet and beg for the job and in return, he would remain passionate all his life for it. But considering the seriousness in Mr. Pillai's tone, he decided to be a mute spectator.

"You were telling me that you can do anything and everything, didn't you?" asked Mr. Pillai.

Having no other choice, Abi shook his head with his eyes facing his feet. He did it so slowly as if he had committed a third-degree murder.

"Well, I am sure not only you but anybody can do any one thing great, but I am also sure that neither you nor anybody can do every other thing okay," said Mr. Pillai.

"I accept that, sir," said Abi trying to escape another head shake.

"I am giving you an opportunity to do one thing great. Let me see what you can do with it," saying this Mr. Pillai handed over a piece of paper to Abi.

The paper was the acknowledgement receipt for the Pizza contest entry which is to be held in a two days' time.

"Seriously?" Abi asked looking at the receipt. "You have registered my name for a pizza making contest?"

"Oh yes, better get ready for it. Tomorrow is going to be one long day for you!" smiled Mr. Pillai.

"But sir, cooking Pizza?" asked Abi in a puzzled tone.

"You have the power to transform yourself into a cook or a scientist provided you have no other choice!" commented Mr. Pillai.

They were silent for a very long time as Abi was a state of shock and refused to make any more comments.

Breaking the silence, Mr. Pillai asked Abi, "So how do you intend to prepare yourself for the competition?"

"Well sir, all I know is that I have to start the day early tomorrow!" said Abi.

After a long walk, both were getting ready for the bed. Abi requested Mr. Pillai to use the bedroom but Mr. Pillai decided against it and told him that he would like to sleep in the balcony much to Abi's surprise.

Abi had set the alarm to 5:00 AM and mentally he was planning to wake up at 6:00 AM. By keeping the alarm at 5:00, he thought he would get an extra buffer to relax, roll and warm up for some more time and also to make up his mind for the 6:00 AM start.

It was 5:00 AM and the alarm rang without a glitch. Abi confirmed the time by looking at the wall clock. He gave a second thought about waking up. He consoled himself saying that an additional 15 minutes of sleep could make him more refreshed for the day ahead. He hit the snooze button and went back to sleep. The next bell was at 5:15 A.M and this time Abi realized that he was too close to that much wanted power nap and therefore he hit the snooze button without any delay. The third bell was at 5:30 AM and Abi was already in his dreams. Without even realizing it, he hit the snooze button again and took the alarm clock in his hand. He kept holding the alarm clock close to himself as he did not want to miss out on the next bell.

The next bell rang, Abi tried to hit the snooze button but the alarm did not go off. Sensing the sound of the bell was in sync with the party music in his dream, he glanced at the clock. He literally jumped out of the bed when he realized it was 8:30 AM. Mr. Pillai was standing near him holding a loud speaker in his hands.

Realizing his mistake, he tried to pacify the much irritated Mr. Pillai with an apologetic smile.

"Get ready soon, you have lots of homework to do!" ordered Mr. Pillai.

Understanding Mr. Pillai's different state of mind today, Abi replied, "Yes sir!"

When Abi entered the hall, he was taken aback at the sight of his room. The hall floor was amazingly clean and so were the walls. For a moment, he had forgotten that it was his house. Mr. Pillai had decorated the house and had changed its entire ambience. Abi kept looking at the intricate details of the room and felt that Mr. Pillai had changed everything in the best way possible.

"When did you do all of this, Sir?" asked Abi in a surprised voice

"Well, I started it when your alarm rang for the first time this morning," said Mr. Pillai.

"I don't know what to say, sir! I don't know if I have to tell say sorry or thanks!" articulated Abi.

"Well, I have done something in a few hours which could have taken you ages. I applied the Zero mind theory and it worked. When I started getting diverted, the loud music helped me to get back on track," explained Mr. Pillai.

Abi stood there acknowledging Mr. Pillai and continued gazing at the refreshing room thinking why he had not thought of it before.

"Get ready soon!" said Mr. Pillai "We have a competition to attend!"

"Sure Sir!" replied Abi with all sincerity.

Abi hurried up and got ready in a jiffy. Realizing it was 9:15 already, he asked Mr. Pillai if they could go out for the breakfast.

"Abi, I have already planned the menu for the entire day today. It will be pizzas all day!" said Mr. Pillai in an interesting voice.

Not understanding how to react, he asked Mr. Pillai, "Pizzas, the whole day?"

"Oh yes, and that too your home made pizzas!" smiled Mr. Pillai.

"Can you help me with it, Sir? I really don't know where to begin!" said Abi with a confused voice.

"Don't begin the journey like a loser. You better stop over-thinking this and start getting focused. So tell me. What do you know about pizza?" asked Mr. Pillai.

Realizing that all he knew about Pizza was how good they tasted and how much they cost. Abi said, "I don't know much about them, sir!"

"Much about what? Answer to the point!" exclaimed Mr. Pillai.

"Much about cooking Pizza, Sir!" answered Abi.

"Now let me ask you a specific question. Who can tell you how to cook a Pizza?" asked Mr. Pillai.

"Maybe someone at the Pizza shop?" said Abi without giving it a thought.

"What if he refuses? Will the world come to an end?" asked Mr. Pillai in a much sarcastic manner.

Understanding that Mr. Pillai was getting annoyed, Abi tried to resort to safety by remaining calm.

"Ask specific questions, you idiot, if you want specific answers!" shouted Mr. Pillai this time.

Trying to ask a specific question this time Abi without a pause said, "What do you need to make a Pizza?"

"Better. So what would be the appropriate second question after it?" asked Mr. Pillai.

"Maybe, how do you make pizza with all that you have!" said Abi.

"So did framing your question help you this time?" asked Mr. Pillai.

"Yes sir, now I think I will resort to the use of internet," said Abi

"Finally!" exclaimed Mr. Pillai, he continued, "Your generation has so much around you and yet you look always lost!"

Abi browsed through all the possible information he could get through internet and took notes. He decided to make a simple vegetarian pizza, understanding that making a non-vegetarian would involve more complexities. He looked at some videos on cooking and decided that his oven was capable of making a pizza. Realizing that he was already late for breakfast, he took a bag and ran to the nearby grocery store.

After buying all the items for the recipe, Abi started working with the dough. It took him a lot of time to gain the right consistency. Once the dough was ready, he started to work on the other aspects. To his surprise, the rest of the process took little time. Within an hour, Abi was ready with his hot pizza.

"Your breakfast is ready, Sir!"

"Good. Bring it on!" said Mr. Pillai.

Abi served the pizza and joined Mr. Pillai for the Breakfast.

"So how do you find the Pizza you made for the first time in your life?" asked Mr. Pillai.

"Not bad for a first timer Sir!" answered Abi.

"But not good enough to win the competition tomorrow," said Mr. Pillai.

"Winning the competition? I hardly thought about it sir. All I am concerned about is giving a good show without any embarrassment," said Abi.

"Let me put it very clearly Abi, if you win this, you are getting the job!" said Mr. Pillai continuing to bite into his pizza.

Shocked at this unexpected comment, Abi said, “Sir this will be too much to expect from a fresher, Sir!”

“Believe me Abi. This job at my company also involves a lot of dimensions, which again will be tough for a fresher!”

Understanding what Mr. Pillai was intending to say, Abi said, “Okay, Sir. I will give it my best shot!”

“So let me get into this competition now. Now as a customer of my Pizza, can you give me feedback?”

“Sure!” replied Mr. Pillai.

“The first thing is that you made me wait for my pizza, which is not good. The faster I get my Pizza, the happier I am. The second thing is that the smell of the Pizza did not excite me. I am not really sure about the freshness of the ingredients. Any stuff is as good as its ingredients are. This theory applies to everything in life, remember!” said Mr. Pillai.

Taking hints from all the feedback, Abi went back to the table to strategize on his next pizza. After a little bit of paperwork, Abi decided to cut down on the Pizza making time by buying a readymade pizza base from the market. He identified places to buy his ingredients, where he was sure about the freshness of the items. As he had to travel a bit to shop, Abi did not want to waste any more time. He left immediately after explaining to Mr. Pillai the ideas he had in his mind.

Abi spent more than two hours shopping. To avoid wasting more time, he filled up his bags with all possible requirements that could arise. He believed that once he has everything he could concentrate only on cooking. He reached home by 2:00 PM. He was way too tired and there was this hungry Mr. Pillai to be fed as well. So without any reprieve, Abi got into action. This time, Abi decided to try out two different recipes which he had learned from the Internet.

“Looks you are well prepared this time!” commented Mr. Pillai.

"I believe so, Sir!" answered Abi continuing to read the recipe.

"All I can say is that my wait for lunch has begun!" said Mr. Pillai understanding that it would pressurize Abi.

"I know, sir! I assure you that I won't make you wait longer this time!" answered Abi.

Going by the rules, Abi worked on both Pizzas at the same time. The first pizza was a tomato special and the second was a mixed vegetable one. Abi added cheese generously this time, believing that it would add more chewiness. Trying to replicate the pizza he saw online, he sliced the vegetables exactly as he saw them in the pictures.

Exactly after 45 minutes of cooking, Abi told Mr. Pillai, "Your Pizza is ready sir!"

"Better timing than before but I still want the wait to be shorter!" said Mr. Pillai.

"I am improving, Sir!"

Tasting the first bite of the Tomato pizza, Mr. Pillai said, "Now I can sense the taste and smell of fresh vegetables here. They add to the taste without much effort from the chef!"

Not trying to argue about his personal effort on the taste, Abi said, "Very true, Sir!"

Abi joined in and their discussion continued.

"How do you find your Pizza this time?" asked Mr. Pillai.

"Well Sir, it is certainly better this time. I believe the readymade Pizza base had helped me concentrate on the other important aspects of cooking," answered Abi.

"That's definitely a good idea. There is no point in wasting time over things for which shortcuts are available. My shortcut philosophy of life is to learn from others mistakes as life is too short to learn everything by oneself!" said Mr. Pillai.

"Very true, Sir!" answered Abi acknowledging the statement.

"Now what's your next plan?" asked Mr. Pillai.

"Well sir, I think I would need to practice a little more and I think I will be ready for the competition!" answered Abi.

"Let me ask you one thing," said Mr. Pillai and continued, "You think you have improved yourself by making these two pizzas. Now what makes you think you have improved?" asked Mr. Pillai.

"Don't you think this Pizza is better than what I made for breakfast?" asked Abi.

"Sure it is. But does that qualify you for the competition? The benchmark you had set for yourself is the first rotten pizza you had made."

"You are right, sir. So what should I do now?" asked Abi.

"Frame your question right, first," answered Mr. Pillai.

Understanding what Mr. Pillai was trying to imply, Abi started to frame specific questions.

After much thought he suddenly shouted, "What should be the benchmark I must set for myself to qualify for the competition?"

"Better. Now you tell me, "What should be the benchmark?" asked Mr. Pillai.

"Well, the benchmark must be the one which is famous and acceptable by all in terms of flavor and ingredients!" answered Abi.

"So do you have any benchmarks in mind?" asked Mr. Pillai.

"Yes sir! There is a small pizza shop down the road. They make amazing pizzas!" answered Abi.

"So now you know what to do next, don't you?" asked Mr. Pillai.

"Sure I do sir. I will buy the vegetarian pizzas from the shop and start comparing them with my own. I will continue to do it till I believe I have equaled it in all possible ways!" answered Abi.

"Well to be a winner you must do more than just equaling it Abi," said Mr. Pillai patting Abi's shoulders.

Understanding that Mr. Pillai was not going to leave him till he delivered the best pizza, Abi skipped his favorite pastime of the day, which was his Happy Lunchtime Nap.

Abi went to the Pizza shop by the road side to buy his benchmark Pizza. The shop was full for lunch and Abi had to wait for one complete hour to buy a pizza of his choice. During this wait, Abi thought all about the techniques involved in making Pizzas. He thought what would happen to the pizza if he started adding things in wrong combinations. His imagination was reaching a different level altogether. At that point, he thought that he would stick to the basics and get a decent entry into the competition. It was 5:30 PM when Abi reached home and he was totally focused on the pizza in hand.

He showed it to Mr. Pillai and told him with a smile, "This is my Idol Pizza. My Pizza will be like this very soon!"

"It looks delicious and you have a long way to go to compete with this!" exclaimed Mr. Pillai.

"I know sir, I am starting right now!" answered Abi and got into the kitchen.

Abi switched on loud music and got into the kitchen, totally focused. He forgot about Mr. Pillai, the job interview, his almost extinct bank balance, his weekend call to his house and memories of his ex-girlfriend. Abi was making two pizzas at the same time. He tasted only a little of the benchmark as he believed he had to keep doing it all day for the comparison. The first batch was ready in no time. Instead of asking Mr. Pillai to taste, Abi took a bite of it himself. He was shocked at its taste. He believed that he had to do a lot more than what he had been doing. He started to make the second set immediately. The second set got ready quicker than Abi anticipated. He tasted them and still felt sad. He believed that he had gotten into an unwanted competition. He got angry and threw the pizzas into the dustbin and came out of the kitchen.

Looking at Mr. Pillai sitting on the sofa, he said, “Sir, looks like I am not fit to be your employee after all. I thought I had it, but now I see that I am too far from getting closer to the benchmark!”

“I don’t think so. I liked the way you made your Pizza for lunch. You better change your strategy, Abi. Don’t keep doing the same thing and keep expecting different results. You have to experiment and you can do it only now. Go back and try out different things even if you trust it or not!” said Mr. Pillai.

This gave Abi some confidence. He went back to the internet and tried to gain all possible information on making pizzas, the properties of pizza constituents, the effect of heat on vegetables and so on. He suddenly felt like he was a pizza scientist. With added insights this time, he got back into the kitchen and started his pizza war.

For the next three hours, Abi was totally immersed in making the pizza. When he thought he had one thing right, another thing was wrong. Despite all the defeats he kept a zero mind and continued to work out various combinations. He made a quick visit to the nearby grocery to fill up the depleting resources.

He also started preparing his own dough for the pizza base as he thought there could be some problem with the readymade pizza base which was preventing him from getting the right taste. All this time, he forgot everything around him. He also missed out on Mr. Pillai who entered the kitchen in the middle of his cooking to grab a pizza for his dinner.

It was 11:30 PM and Abi had made the 18th pizza for the day. He looked at it. There was hardly any difference between it and the benchmark. With all keenness and fear, he took a bite of it. He felt he was swallowing happiness. It was just like the benchmark! He wanted to shout out loud at the world that finally “he did it”.

Taking the rest of the pizza, he rushed to serve it to Mr. Pillai. But Mr. Pillai was already asleep.

Not wanting to disturb Mr. Pillai, Abi kept the remaining portion of the Pizza in the refrigerator for the next day. Abi felt a sense of accomplishment after a long time in his life. With his mind focused on the next day's competition, Abi was revising the final recipe of success in his mind.

❁❁❁

It was 4:00 AM in the morning. Mr. Pillai tried to wake up Abi.

"Abi, wake up. We have an important place to go to!" said Mr. Pillai removing his blanket.

Thinking he was late again, Abi jumped out of the bed in a hurry. He looked at the clock and was worried.

"But Sir, it is just 4:00 AM!" said Abi in a merciful voice.

"I know that. You have 20 minutes to get ready. We have an important place to go to!"

Not trying to think hard, Abi got ready in the given time.

It was 4:30 AM when they started out on their journey in a cab hired by Mr. Pillai on the previous day itself.

It was around 6:00 AM when they reached the base of a small hill at the outskirts of the city. Abi started to gaze at the place with amazement. The place was masked with greenery and birds of all kinds were chirping around. The sight of the early morning sun over the hill looked like heaven to Abi. He was regretting that he had not brought the camera to capture this beauty.

"Come on, let's move!" said Mr. Pillai marching towards a pathway.

"But where are we going?" asked Abi in excitement.

"Follow me and you will find out!" answered Mr. Pillai not bothering to wait for Abi.

After walking for 15 minutes towards the hill, they saw a small hut amidst a flower garden just at the foot of the hill.

"Beautiful!" exclaimed Abi looking at the pretty robust hut.

"Well, it's been here for more than a century now!" said Mr. Pillai

"Are you serious?" asked Abi.

"Yes I am!" said Mr. Pillai. He said, "This is not just a hut. It is the only restaurant in this locality. It opens at 4:00 AM and runs till 11:00 PM. It used to serve food to the workers working at the mines on the other side of the hill. Now since the quarry had limited their operation, the restaurant thrives mostly by travelers who pass this location!"

"That's interesting," said Abi. "How do you know about this place?" he asked.

"Well, I used to work in that mine during my early years!" answered Mr. Pillai with a hint of nostalgia.

Abi stood silent. He was amazed by the answer. He wanted to ask more about it but restricted himself as he saw Mr. Pillai moving towards the hut. A couple of workers were having their breakfast outside the hut. They were sitting under the shade of the dense trees in front of the hut. The elevated roots of the trees served as the furniture for the hill restaurant along with some old tables.

An old man came up to Mr. Pillai and asked "What can I get for you?"

Mr. Pillai answered, "What else will I ask other than the famous bread rolls and the tomato- chili sauce from your kitchen!"

"As you wish, Sir!" said the old man.

"One more thing, can you heat this bread for me, please?" requested Mr. Pillai to the old man handing over the pizza which Abi had made the earlier night.

Abi smiled at Mr. Pillai signifying his thanks and love to Mr. Pillai.

"I believe this is the best restaurant I have ever visited!" said Mr. Pillai.

"This place is amazing!" said Abi in an excited voice. He continued, "There is plenty of greenery all around. The flowers are beautiful and I am sure you must have a lot of memories associated with this place for sure!"

"You are right. The thing which amazes me is that this restaurant is self sufficient by itself. All the vegetables, fruits and the spices needed for the restaurant are grown here." said Mr. Pillai.

"Here is your bread roll with sauce and here is your own hot bread sir!" said the old man handing over the plates to Mr. Pillai.

"Thank you very much!" said Abi as he started to dig into his plates.

The very first bite of the bread roll with the sauce made Abi's eye open wide. He was not able to believe that a simple sauce could make the food that delicious. He continued his digging and enjoyed every bit of that food.

Meanwhile, Mr. Pillai also tasted Abi's Pizza along with his favorite sauce.

"Do you know why I brought you here?" asked Mr. Pillai to Abi.

"Maybe to give some final lessons before my contest today?" answered Abi.

"True to some extent but the final lessons will not be from me but from the old lady inside the hut!" said Mr. Pillai.

Mr. Pillai called on the old man and detailed him about the competition that Abi was about to take part in.

The old man smiled at Abi and said, “Get your cooking lessons from my wife and before you leave this place make sure you are fully loaded with our garden vegetables!”

“Thank you very much, Sir!” said Abi. He felt like a little joyous kid with concerned teachers all around him.

The old man guided Abi into the hut and introduced him to his wife. He also told her about the competition that Abi was having later that day.

“I am not good at explaining cooking but you can see the way I cook!” said the old lady starting to cook the bread roll.

“Can you show me how to make the sauces as well?” asked Abi

“Sure!” said the old lady and got back to work.

The first thing that Abi noticed was the way the old lady cut the vegetable and seasoned them before using it in the bread. He was also taking note of all the spices that were being used for the preparation. Once the bread roll was done, the old lady started to prepare the sauce. She took the fresh tomatoes and the chilies from her basket and started to cut them. The colours of the vegetables were way too sharp compared to the one Abi used in his Pizza the earlier day. The old lady added a homemade concentrate for the sauce. Abi without hesitation got the recipe for the concentrate. The old lady kept speaking about her sons, grandchildren during her course of cooking.

At one point of time she looked at Abi and said, “The first time I made this sauce was for my grandson. It’s only because of him, that I have developed different recipes apart from the regular conventional ones!”

“So where is he now?” asked Abi.

“He has gone overseas long time back and since then he did not even call me once!” cried the old lady.

"Did you try to contact him? Abi asked.

"How?" asked the old lady. She continued, "All our children have deserted us for a better life and I have no clue of anyone's whereabouts!"

The old lady continued with her story. Abi started feeling sorry for the poor lady. He wanted to comfort her somehow, but he knew that the only thing he could do to solace her is to listen to her story and her struggles.

After a couple of hours' stay, Mr. Pillai and Abi decided to start back for home. Abi thanked them personally and got their blessings. Before Abi could get into the taxi, the old lady called Abi inside the hut and gave him a big bottle of the sauce concentrate.

"This will help you in your competition!" said the old lady with wet eyes.

"I don't know what to say but believe me, you got a new grandson today. I will visit you every weekend and we shall create new recipes all over again!" said Abi in an emotional tone.

"I will wait then!" the old lady said with tears rolling down her eyes.

The taxi started its journey back to the city. Abi was totally blown away by the series of events. He kept thinking about the old lady and how similar she was to his own grandmother. He also started to think about all the special food his grandma prepared for him and also the way she manipulated it to please his taste buds.

The taxi reached Abi's house at 11:30 AM. The competition was to start at 4:00 PM and all the contestants had to get their pizza to the judges' table before 4:00 PM. Having sufficient time on hand, Abi decided to go slow and steady for the event. He started to mentally prepare. He started to write the steps to follow and what he could improve. He spent some time cleaning the kitchen and getting the groceries in place. He did not want to start cooking early as he believed it would reduce the freshness of the pizza by the time he took it to the judges. Meanwhile, he decided to take a quick walk to his roadside pizza shop and buy one of his vegetarian pizzas for his comparative study later. Mr. Pillai too joined him for the walk.

When they reached the pizza shop, they saw that it was closed. On enquiry from the nearby shop, they learnt that the restaurant owner Joe had taken the day off to participate in a Pizza making competition.

"Oh my God! Looks like I will have tough competition!" said Abi concerned over Joe's participation.

"If you think Joe is your only competition, then give it a thought. Almost half of this town is participating in this competition!" said Mr. Pillai.

"How do you know that?" asked Abi.

"I was the one who stood in the queue to register your name!" answered Mr. Pillai.

Abi grew silent. He felt weak and all the confidence he had gained from the previous day drained out. He started to worry about the other competitors, their experiences and their influence over the judges. He started to get back to his old thinking habits when Mr. Pillai interrupted him.

"Are you afraid?" asked Mr. Pillai.

"I am," answered Abi in a low voice.

"It is true that this competition is important for you for more than one reason but let me tell you worrying can never help you in any way!" said Mr. Pillai.

"I understand. But do I have any other choice?" asked Abi.

"Worrying can only hamper a positive outcome. If you can do something to win, do it rather than worrying and if you have nothing to do about it then move on. Anyway, worry is the favorite pastime of a loser!" answered Mr. Pillai.

"It is easy to say that but my mind keeps getting back to it. What do you think I can do about it?" asked Abi again.

"Think of something good that has happened to you or that can happen to you. Your body will experience the same feeling of happiness by releasing the happy chemicals and that can make you relax and rejuvenated. I should warn you that if you think of anything bad that has happened to you or that can happen to you, the body will experience the sadness and thereby make you more stressful!" explained Mr. Pillai.

Over the course of their discussion, both Mr. Pillai and Abi ate at a small beachside restaurant. Abi kept thinking about the Mountain Hut restaurant that they had visited in the morning and the old lady reminded him of his grandmother. Abi could not be with his grandma during her final days and he felt bad for not taking care of his grandma when she needed him the most. He was thinking that the agony his grandma must have gone through must be similar to the one the old lady was experiencing now.

After lunch, Abi walked back home, whereas Mr. Pillai preferred to stay at the beach for some more time. Abi reached home at exactly 2:00 PM. The contest venue was hardly a kilometer away from Abi's house. Considering the time to be ideal to begin his cooking, Abi started to arrange items in the kitchen. He decided to make two pizzas at one go and then he would choose the best one for the contest. He started to prepare dough for one of the pizza base and used the readymade pizza base for the other. He cut up the fresh vegetables from the hills. The fresh aroma from the vegetables reminded him of the greenery of the hills. Thinking of the beauty of the place he visited, he continued to cook. He felt he had mastered the art finally. After putting the Pizzas in the oven, he started to create the magical sauce he had learned earlier that day. Although he knew that people would not use sauce for pizza, he continued with its preparation as he was very impressed with its taste. He used the old lady's sauce concentrate economically as he wanted to treasure it for a long time. He remembered the mixed vegetable sauce his grandma used to make for him. Abi hated vegetables when he was a kid. She would make a mixed vegetable sauce and would conceal it in Abi's favorite Aloo Parathas. She would make little holes on the top of the Paratha and pour little sauce into it. Unaware of this Abi continued to enjoy his Parathas. The truth came out one day when his over ambitious Grandma added more sauce into the Parathas thereby spoiling the party. Smiling at the happy memories, Abi continued his sauce preparation. The sauce was ready in no time. He tasted it and found it was almost similar to the one he tasted in the morning.

Now came the important part of the day. He slowly removed the pizzas from the oven and kept them on the table. The looks were not up to his expectation but he assured himself that the taste would compensate for that. He tried touching the top of one of the pizza and found it to be too hard. Sensing fear, he touched the other pizza, it was also similar. Not wanting to wait anymore, he took a bite at one of the pizza and found it to be way too dry. Abi was stunned. He was unable to understand where he had gone wrong. He tried to taste the other pizza and the result was similar.

Abi started to panic. It was already 3:15 PM and his pizzas were as brittle as a pappad. Abi was not sure what he had to do next. Abi found the taste good, however, the dryness has taken away all the charm. He thought if he showed the judges this, they may just reject it outright because of the dryness. Not thinking any more, Abi gathered his wits and started making the next set. This time, he thought that the addition of extra cheese would do the trick. He continued to work at a greater speed, trying not to fear the competition.

Working like a sprinter, he finished the pizza base in no time. He put the pizza in the oven and started praying for its success. It was 3:40 PM when Abi took the pizza out of the oven. It looked the same. Abi could not believe his eyes. He kept wondering where he had gone wrong. A heavy feeling started setting in him.

He felt like everything was lost. Tears started pouring out of his eyes. He wanted to run away from everything and yet he could not. He was not able to stand in the kitchen anymore. He rushed out of the kitchen. He saw Mr. Pillai standing in the balcony.

Abi went directly to Mr. Pillai and said, “I am a loser, Sir! You shouldn’t hire me. I am sorry I wasted your time. I let you down and the trust you had in me. I am sorry sir. Please forgive me!”

“Slow down Abi! What happened?” asked Mr. Pillai.

“Sir, my pizza looks like dry bread and I can hardly present it in the competition!” said Abi.

“Let me see it,” said Mr. Pillai and went inside the Kitchen as Abi followed him.

After looking at the pizzas, Mr. Pillai took a bite of the first batch.

“But this tastes delicious!” said Mr. Pillai.

“Sir, please stop pleasing me. I know how a good pizza tastes and feels!” said Abi.

“Well, in that case, you make a special pizza and not just a good pizza!” said Mr. Pillai.

“What do you mean sir?” asked Abi.

“If you are sure that your Pizza is not up to the regular standards then better create a new standard, Abi,” said Mr. Pillai.

“But sir, it is already too late!” said Mr. Pillai.

“Well it is always the last moments that make the difference!” commented Mr. Pillai.

After saying this Mr. Pillai went back to the hall trying to catch up with the day’s newspaper.

Abi was confused. He was not able to make out anything of what Mr. Pillai had suggested.

He went back to Mr. Pillai and asked, “Can you give me a clue?”

"Like I told you once, to think out of the box you have to become a kid," said Mr. Pillai and got back to his paper.

"Think like a kid?" Abi asked. "If I have to think like a kid, I have to become a kid. So why not think about the days when I was a kid. Can that help me?"

Abi suddenly remembered the Aloo Parathas his grandma used to make for him. He also thought about the vegetable sauce she had concealed in his Parathas.

Then he thought loudly, "Why not I conceal my sauces in my Pizza? This way I am ensuring the dryness of the Pizza is reduced and I am also ensuring my sauces are tasted! But how can I conceal my sauce in the pizza, it's too difficult to drill into its surface!"

Thinking this he just glanced at his project work for his Ph.D., the "Nano driller".

He felt numb for a second. He felt everything around him is happening for a reason. He could not control his excitement. He took his Nano driller and tried to drill on the first set of discarded pizza. It worked like magic. He could put in small, identical and deep holes on the dry surface of the Pizza. Abi could not control his excitement and jumped with joy.

Without wasting any more time, he drilled in identical, evenly spaced holes in the best looking pizza of the lot. With the help of a syringe which he had kept for his project work, he started filling the sauce into the pizza. He filled the tomato and chili sauce alternatively in the tiny holes. When he was done with it, the pizza looked totally different and that made him realize that he had set a way different benchmark this time.

It was already 3:55 PM and Abi realized he has not a second to waste. Packing his pizza in a box, he rushed out of the house pulling Mr. Pillai along. He shouted at the passing cab to stop by and jumped into it. By the time Abi reached the venue, it was already 4:10 PM. Without a second thought, he rushed to the registration counter. The receptionist at the counter refused to admit Abi as he was late for the event. That was when the interesting thing happened. Abi started to weep like a kid. His weeping got louder and louder. The weeping started to gain the attention of the nearby people. They started to gather around. Realizing the problem, everyone requested the receptionist to make an exception. Not able to cope up with all the requests, she finally succumbed. She gave Abi the admit card asked him to rush into the event hall.

Once Abi reached the hall, he saw hundreds of people standing beside their pizza. Abi took the vacant corner table and placed his pizza on the table with utmost care. After placing the pizza, he realized that he was standing next to Joe, the pizza maker.

Looking at Abi's pizza, Joe commented "What happened to your pizza, Chicken Pox?"

Abi without any concern replied, "Yes, but a colorful one!"

The judges had started their tasting sessions. Abi felt his Pizza would be the last one to be tasted as he was standing in the last possible corner. It was already 4:30 PM and the judges had to give the result before 5:30 PM as per schedule. They started rushing up their tasting. When they reached Abi, they suddenly stopped to look at his Pizza. After looking at hundreds of pizzas, it was only Abi's pizza which stood apart from the conventional look.

"What do we have here?" asked one of the senior judges taking a piece of the Pizza.

"Sir, I believe this would be the pizza I would have wanted as a kid!" answered Abi.

After tasting the pizza, the judge remained silent for a moment keeping his eyes closed.

"Good!" he commented and started to move away from Abi's table.

Unable to determine anything from the judge's comment, Abi kept looking on at his dotted pizza.

The tasting sessions were over and the contestants were made to wait in the hall to know the result of the competition.

Abi wanted to call Mr. Pillai inside the hall but the entry was restricted only to the contestants.

It was almost 5:45 PM when the Judges took the stage. They got seated in their respective seats and started discussing among themselves.

After some discussion, one of the female judges took the podium and started to speak about the competition and its success.

Next came another female judge who explained the judging criteria. She was elaborating on various details, some of which Abi had not even thought of. After her speech, Abi made up his mind to get away from the hall, however the keenness to know the winner of the competition made him stay for some more time.

Finally, the senior judge took to the podium to declare the winners.

"Let me declare the winners starting from the third place. The third place goes to Mr. Joe Fernandez!" the judge announced.

Abi instantly looked at Joe. Joe was disappointed. He was anticipating the first place. However, with the crowd cheering his name, he smiled and reached the stage to collect his prize.

"The second place goes to Mrs. Jayanthi Mohan," announced the judge.

"Mrs. Jayanthi Mohan has amazed me in more than one way. Her presentation of the pizza, the perfect combination of the ingredients and the softness of the crust had almost made it to the top," said the judge. After handing over the prize to Mrs. Jayanthi, the judge went back to the podium to announce the winner. The judge said, "Ladies and Gentlemen, now comes the climax: the declaration of the winner. Before I announce the winner, I have something to tell you all. Like you all know, everyone is a kid at heart. No matter how old or how successful a person becomes, he remains a kid at heart. It is his or her childhood memories that bring solace to them irrespective of its differences. In this context, I would say I had a flash of my childhood with a little bite of pizza today. This winning pizza might not have the sophistication of a commercial pizza but it definitely had a piece of childhood in those little holes on that otherwise dry crust. So Ladies and Gentlemen, please put your hands together to the young winner of today's competition, Mr. Abhinav Sharma!"

The audience gave a huge applause and tried to locate Abhinav in the crowd. Abi stood there; still unable to digest what had just happened. He felt a unique silence amidst all the cheers and applause. Tears of happiness dropped on the chicken pox pizza. Trying to control his emotions, Abi started walking towards the stage. He could hardly react to the wishes he received on his way to the stage. On reaching the stage, he was handed over the winner's trophy on which it was engraved "The Pizza Champion".

Looking at Abi, the senior Judge smiled and said, "Good job, son, looks like the world is all yours today. Go ahead and take the podium as well!"

"Thank you, sir!" Abi said and reached the podium to address the audience. Standing on stage, Abi smiled with a great sense of relief and started speaking.

"I feel like I am still in the kitchen. It feels amazing to be standing here. I wish I had felt this before. I was searching for the exit gate before the announcement of the results, actually! I have been at the podium many times before this as a student but today it is totally different. If you had known me before, then you would have know that I would be the last one you would approach for making a pizza, but that doesn't mean that you can approach me now. I am still learning. All my life I have been a chaser of dreams which unfortunately was never mine. I was trying to live as somebody else, in my disguise. It was only when an old man came to me and said, "Son, wake up, you are already a big fat loser. You better know yourself first before the world knows you!" Thanks to him, I am here today in front of you all as a winner!"

After receiving accolades from the audience, Abi made way out of the event hall in search of Mr. Pillai.

Abi was in an ecstatic mood. He wanted to see Mr. Pillai and show him the trophy like a kid. He kept searching for Mr. Pillai but he could not find him. It was then that he realized that he didn't have his mobile number. He remembered that he had never seen Mr. Pillai with a mobile phone. After all these confusing thoughts and no trace of Mr. Pillai, Abi walked out of the building. As he walked, Abi felt that someone was pulling his pants from behind. Expecting it to be Mr. Pillai, he turned around in a jiffy to see a little kid pulling Abi's trousers.

The kid looked at Abi and asked, "Are you the winner today?"

With a curious smile Abi answered," Yes, looks like that!"

"Then this one is for you!" said the kid handing over a letter to Abi.

Not waiting for Abi's response, the kid sprinted away. Abi opened the letter and found it to be from Mr. Pillai. It was a two-page letter, written by hand. Abi settled down below a neem tree to read the letter.

Dear Abi,

My two days with you were special to me. Thank you for all the respect and hospitality you offered me. I will be always grateful to you for it. I am writing this to convey something which I could not tell you in person. I know it is difficult to give directions to today's youth, but it is also difficult for today's old ones to stop giving it. So please try to find a nice place to sit down so that you can read it fully and patiently.

The first time I saw you at the beach, I immediately understood that you were under stress. Your sleepless face and dark circles indicated that you are going through a bad phase. You were immersed in your own worries and all my words that time fell on deaf ears. I wanted to know you and your problems. That was when I decided to stay with you.

The first thing anybody will notice about you is your weight and I am pretty sure that you are very much conscious about that. You are sincere worrying about it rather than doing something about it. The very example of you keeping your clock 15 minutes faster and you using the snooze button indicates your preparedness towards the inefficiencies of your life. Your act of postponement is not only killing your present but also your future as well. Never get the disease of thinking about that one day which can change your fortunes, start living that day today.

About your way of approach to things, I want to give you two interesting examples that had happened in front of your own eyes. You had not given any thought about these incidents, but believe me; Nature has his own way of conveying messages. The first incident was the taxi guy who had put on the right indicator to turn left. His excuse as you know was that his left indicator wasn't working. The same is the problem with you. Just because you are good at one thing, you cannot expect to win everything with that same good thing. Different things need different outlooks and for that, you need to learn something new and unlearn something old. If you mess up with it, you will end up in an accident.

The second example is the mysterious dead sparrow in front of your house. There was no mystery in the bird's death. The poor thing has been trying to get away from the building block by repeatedly dashing at the glass window mistaking it for an open space. This incidentally resulted in its death. Similar to the Sparrow, you are a repetitive task master. This was imminent in your initial attempt to cook pizza. Any failure at any stage needs to be introspected. If you persist without making any change to the approach, then your effort will end up like the sparrow. Success results from a focused creative pursuit rather than an emotional repetitive approach. I would say too much education has left you with a narrow imagination. You believe things should be well defined to the world otherwise it is wrong. However, in reality, it is not the truth but it is a manmade illusion. Once you get enslaved to these set of rules and beliefs, you will miss out on the beauty of life. Your final pizza is the proof of breaking the conventions and still being good enough to win the odds.

One of the interesting aspects about you is that you are a multi-specialty man. You have imbibed different knowledge and different skills. But you hardly had converted this specialty of yours into your strengths. In fact, you have allowed people to assume that with this variety of qualifications, you have missed out on the focus on life. I am telling you in this letter that multi-specialty is indeed the need of the hour. A knowledgeable person is the one who can only understand and imbibe knowledge. A practical person is the one who can only apply this knowledge to his everyday life. Whereas a successful person is the one who can manipulate his knowledge of anything into everything. The very example of this is your nano driller working on your winning pizza. With varied specialty, you have lots to choose rather than sitting on a single skill.

The next thing I want to tell you is to stop pacifying people by compromising on your ideas. I want to tell you about a young friend of mine. This guy was a film maker. He started his career by making movies on totally unconventional themes. His screenplay, camera and dialogues were all a lot different from those making conventional cinema. Slowly, his talent got recognized and he was roped in by producers to make movies for them. When he started becoming famous, the expectations from him also began increasing. This increased the budgets for the movie. With so much money at stake, producers believed that the movie must entertain the masses so that their money would be recovered with profit. For this reason my friend had started to rethink his ideas to suit the masses. This continued to happen repeatedly for his next set of movies. Today, this guy has lost his originality in a quest for satisfying the masses. He is no more looked as special. I don't want this to happen to you.

During my stay with you, I realized that you dream too much and dream too big. I am not against thinking big and having big dreams but having too little to start with can hamper your confidence and reduce your happiness. You should set moving targets for every fortnight. You might start your game like an amateur, but when you keep playing consistently and keep improving your strokes every day, then one fine day you will start beating the champions.

I must tell you that today the world is filled with mediocre people. They set the limits and live within their comfort zones. But to be a winner, the first thing you must do is to count the non-comfort zones every day. The more they are, the closer you are to victory. Never save the best effort for the last, let every effort of yours be like your last one and let that last effort begin now.

Finally, I have to tell you something which might come as a shock to you. I am not Mr. Pillai and I am sorry for cheating you on this. I really believed you needed more than just a job and this made me take the decision of becoming Mr. Pillai. Please don't try to find me, as I will send you an invitation to meet me at an appropriate time.

With Love,

Mr. Pillai

THE MESSENGER

Before 3 years

"Dude, are you sure?" Ajay asked opening his third beer for the night.

"100 percent, dude, I know it by the way she looks at me," answered Deepak who was holding his fourth.

"Then why don't you propose to her? The world is already running out of single girls."

"Come on, I just don't want to rush. Anyway Priya is made for me and nothing can separate her from me," replied Deepak.

"Dude, you are really drunk now. You better go to sleep and let me enjoy the party alone," said Ajay who was tired of Deepak's repetitive love tales.

"Come on Aju, you are my savior. Give me some ideas."

"You are asking the wrong guy. I have been single all my life and some even think I am gay. Thanks to our night walks around the campus, we are already a hot couple among our juniors."

"Stop joking man, I am serious."

"In that case don't wait for an ideal time but make any time ideal for you. Trust me, I really mean what I say," said Ajay.

Deepak kept thinking about what Ajay had just said and suddenly shouted, "In that case can I ask her to join me for the jog tomorrow!"

"Good one, but tell me when was the last time you jogged in your life."

"That's immaterial, when I can die for her then why can't I jog for her?"

"Dude, it is high time you hand over your beer to me. I am yet to get high because of your stupid talk."

"Okay, okay, I got it. I am sending her a message so she can join me for the jog."

"Whatever. But remember, it is 1:00 AM already!" sighed Aju, finishing the rest of the drink in the can in a single gulp. Paying no heed to what Ajay was saying, Deepak texted Priya saying, "Will you join me for a jog tomorrow?"

After sending the message, Deepak kept looking at his cell phone eagerly for a reply. "Stop staring at it, dude, it's not our communications teacher!" shouted Ajay.

"Okay, fine! Stop giving Gyan and give back my beer!"

With an annoyed expression, Ajay returned the beer thinking that he should have left Deepak alone with his mobile.

After a couple of sips, both Deepak and Ajay were in seventh heaven and they could hardly hold their cans.

Deepak's phone beeped, signaling the arrival of a message.

It took nearly five minutes for Deepak to realize that there was a text message for him and another five minutes to open it.

The message read: "ok sure, 6:00 in the morning at the tennis court!"

Deepak was too intoxicated to express his real feelings, but he was very clear that the jog on the next day will be the jog of his life.

"Aju, we are going for the jog tomorrow!" shouted Deepak lying on his stomach.

"Why me, idiot? Let me die in peace here!" Aju shouted back, now finally drunk.

"Because you are my friend, my philosopher and my guide and my... "

"You better stop with that man, not a word more than that. Sometimes I really doubt my sexual orientation!"

"So are you coming, then?"

"Okay, but I am not running. It's against my principles."

"Thank you Man, I love you."

"Ass @#$%!"

❁❁❁

Deepak set the alarm for 5:45 AM and dozed off when he realized that the alarm was already ringing.

"What the F!@#$? Aju why the hell did you set the alarm?" shouted Deepak still intoxicated.

"Dude, what are you talking about? I thought it was you this time!" said Aju letting the alarm ring continuously.

"But why is it always me? You better switch off the alarm before I switch off you!" said Deepak trying to get back to sleep.

"Now I remember, today is your admission day in the jogging class. You better decide what is important to you, girlfriend or sleep?" said Aju in a drowsy state.

"Man, that is a million dollar question. If you had asked me the same question some one year ago, I would have said sleep and today my answer would be Zzzzzzz…" Deepak dozed off again with the alarm still humming in the background.

"Good decision, man, you understood life very soon. Girlfriends can come any time but the early morning sleep can come only in the early mornings."

"Did you say morning?" Deepak panicked and jumped out of bed. "I might miss my opportunity to propose to her!" he continued.

"Good God! Leave it dude. Don't worry, when God is with you who can be against you?" murmured Aju in his sleepy state.

"You are right, man. You are my God now and only you can guide me in my happy and sad days!" exclaimed Deepak and pulled Aju off of the bed.

Aju crashed on the floor. After the fall, he looked at Deepak and asked "What happy days were you talking about?"

After a quick crow bath, Deepak got ready for the jog in his gym suit which he had tried only once in the dressing room. That was two years ago before joining the business school.

"Dude, you look Hot!" said Aju in a funny tone as Deepak was spraying Aju's deodorant in his mouth that too after gargling with mouthwash thrice.

"Thanks man, I always thought red suits me!"

Ajay in a low voice replied, "I think it's more of pinkish. But otherwise your eyes are really red!"

"Are you serious? You really think so? Thank you, man! You are my savior again!" Deepak exchanged his gym suit with Ajay's and rushed to the tennis court. Ajay kept staring at the pink suit for a very long time before he succumbed to wearing it.

❁❁❁

Outside, it was still dark and there was not a single soul to be seen. Both Deepak and Ajay walked slowly towards the tennis court and sat on the bench.

"Dude, I think 6:00 AM is the middle of the night to everybody else as well. It's time for us to get back to our room and regain our right to sleep!" said Aju rubbing his eyes.

Aju's words fell on deaf ears. Deepak pulled out his cell phone to take a look at the time. He was shocked to find that it was 4:00 AM. Deepak had mistakenly kept the alarm at 3:45 AM instead of 5:45 AM. This did not deter Deepak to stay, as he felt that he would be sucked back into sleep if he went back to his room. Ajay was already sleeping on the bench.

At around 6:30 AM, Priya reached the Tennis Court in her pure white shorts.

Seeing Priya approach, Deepak tried to assemble his jumbled hair and woke up Aju in a hurry.

"You guys are here already? I thought boys are always late for a morning jog!" said Priya stretching her arms.

"I believe in early morning exercise and I arise before the sun everyday!" said Deepak without a hitch thereby executing his well rehearsed line.

Ajay did not say a word but continued to look at the ground as if mother earth wanted him to sleep on her lap.

"So who is this?" asked Priya pointing at Aju.

"Oh, I forgot to introduce him! He is Ajay, my friend. He is a fitness freak like me and by the way he wanted me to teach him yoga!"

"That's great. By the way why are both your eyes red?" asked Priya

"We just completed uparasana, which increases our blood flow to the eyes which makes it look red!" said Deepak.

"What the hell?" Aju thought.

"Please teach me some of the postures when you are free. Shall we jog now?" asked Priya.

"Sure, let's start!" replied Deepak.

"You guys proceed. I have to perfect some of my postures I just learned!" said Aju in a hurry thereby not allowing Deepak to force him to run with a hangover.

"Okay then! Let's move, Deepak!" said Priya as she continued to jog without waiting for Deepak.

Deepak looked at Aju angrily and started to follow Priya. Aju on the other hand, was moving to the bench, which for the day seemed like the best invention ever made.

Deepak couldn't concentrate on his running as he felt like he was being pulled toward a side of the road. When he tried to correct it, he felt like he was being pulled on the other side. Priya was annoyed by the slow pace and unique running style of Deepak. She asked, "Why are you running sideward?"

Deepak thought, "To me, everybody else is running sideward!" but he said to Priya. "It is proved scientifically that running sideward in a slow speed burns more calories than it does with a quick sprint!"

"Are you serious? How do you know that?" Priya asked in surprise.

"Why so many questions? My brain is still in coma!" Deepak thought. Aloud, he replied, "My gym instructor told me when I was teaching him yoga!"

"Great, you seem to be a real fitness freak, I love your attitude!" said Priya and began to jog further.

"And I love your everything!" Deepak said in his mind.

After an hour of Jogging, Priya slowed down on her speed and started to walk whereas Deepak's eyeballs were ready to pop out along with last night's dinner. However, he never showed out any discomfort and continued to be in the hunt for Priya's love. Both Priya and Deepak walked slowly towards the tennis court to finish their jog. Once they reached the spot, they noticed Aju lying upside down on the bench, snoring loudly.

"So is this any kind of a posture you had taught him?" asked Priya hiding her smile.

Deepak decided not to answer any more questions and replied with a 32-teeth smile.

Walking past Aju, Deepak asked Priya about her plans for the day.

"Nothing much, first temple then a movie!" she said slowly, looking for the reaction on Deepak's face.

"That sounds great, can I join you for the movie?" asked Deepak instantly without a thought.

"Only if you join me at the temple!" said Priya and continued to walk to her hostel without saying bye.

❁❁❁

With a hangover and a headache, Deepak reached the temple without Aju.

"Aju nobody is here. Looks like I am first here as well!" Deepak texted Aju.

"Great, Dude, Priya will think that you are first in everything!" replied Aju.

"Hmm... will text you once she comes!" messaged Deepak.

Deepak sat down at the temple entrance checking his breath once every five minutes.

He leaned against the temple wall and closed his eyes. He slowly drifted into a deep sleep when Priya woke him up.

"Were you sleeping?" she asked hiding her smile.

"No I was meditating!" he thought, but instead he said, "Yah, sort of!"

"Are your eyes always red or are they red only today?" asked Priya.

"Looks like the interview session has already started!" thought Deepak. "I didn't sleep properly yesterday. Maybe that's why. Anyway shall we go for the prayer now?" he asked.

"Sure, but before that I want you to do something for me!" Priya said.

"Come on, throw it on me. I will leave my education, my parents, my friends and everything for you!" thought Deepak, but said, "Tell me, Priya!"

"Actually I am supposed to recite the mantras and slogans from this book before I do the prayer. I do this on all Sundays. But my throat is bad today, so I wanted you to recite it for me so that I can directly go for the prayer!" asked Priya.

"I can hardly speak with this intoxicating hangover and now you ask me to recite this book of tongue twisters? Are you kidding me?" Deepak thought. "Sure why not? But I need some help," said Deepak.

"Don't worry about that, I shall make arrangements for it!" saying these words Priya left the place and disappeared.

"She asked me to recite mantras☹" Deepak texted Aju.

"Good God, I am not with you, otherwise you would have made me a Pujari!" came the reply.

"Stop joking, Dude! Tell me. What should I do?"

"Listen. Tell me, who will check you? Just read a little in the lowest volume possible and pretend as if you just completed it whenever she returns!"

"Good One!" Deepak replied.

Just when Deepak was about to start his low volume reading, a lean Pujari with a mike approached him.

"Deepak?" he asked pointing at Deepak.

"Yah!" answered Deepak with a question mark in his face.

"Good, come with me, we are already late!" said the Pujari grabbing Deepak's hand and rushed him towards a lecture hall.

"But late for what?" asked Deepak with his red eyes getting more reddish.

The Pujari brought Deepak in front a wide audience who had gathered at the lecture hall to listen to Guruji's talk.

Deepak's face went pale and with red eyes he looked like a frozen Dracula brought under sun.

"Sit down, beta!" a calm voice came from the centre of the hall. It was the Guruji who had advised him to sit near him.

"I will tell you the meaning and significance of the mantras which this young man will recite in pure Sanskrit!" said Guruji looking at the gathering.

"What is happening?" Deepak began to tremble.

Despite the silent crowd sitting around, he texted, "Dude, I am in deep shit. I have to read the mantras to some hundred people sitting around me!"

"Is Priya there? She must be really impressed. You are hitting the bull's eye every time, Dude!"

"Ass H!@#" Deepak texted back.

"Can we start son?" asked Swamiji.

"Sure Sir!" answered Deepak.

"Now read the first two lines of Chapter one loudly," said Swamiji.

"Man this is getting tougher. He wants me to read them loudly too!" texted Deepak.

"Then do it, dude. You have nothing to worry about. It's their problem. It's God's wish to make them listen to a drunkard's blabber!"

"Okay then!" Deepak replied back.

The first two lines of the first chapter resembled a jumble crossword to Deepak. Irrespective of the concern, he loudly dictated the first line with stern confidence. There was pin drop silence after his dictation. Then Guruji slowly picked the book from Deepak and checked for the lines. Guruji smiled to himself and asked Deepak to repeat the lines. Deepak did it with more confidence this time. This time, both Guruji and the crowd burst out laughing. Deepak was not sure what to do, so he continued to read aloud. The crowd's laughter started getting louder and louder. After almost 15 minutes of nonstop laughter, Swamiji asked Deepak to stop reading and said, "So far, I was aware only of the meaning of these mantras but today I realized the amount humor contained in them! Thanks to you, son. You made a statement today!"

Not sure of how to react to the statement, Deepak thanked Guruji and slowly walked out. The crowd gave him a loud round of applause as he walked out of the hall. Deepak was happy within and wondered how, by doing something wrong, something good had happened. He saw Priya approaching him from a distance. He immediately opened the book and pretended to read.

"You haven't read them till now?" asked Priya.

"No, I was reading them slowly. By the way, did you send anyone to dictate the lines to Swamiji?" asked Deepak.

"What Swamiji?" I didn't get you!" replied Priya.

"Nothing, nothing, leave it," replied Deepak not able to understand what just happened.

"Anyway, sit here and finish reading. I will get some Prasad from the temple!" said Priya and disappeared once again.

"What am I doing here?" Deepak cursed his fate. After a while, he saw Priya returning with Prasad, he slipped to the last page of the book and pretended to read. As Priya came closer, devotees at the conference hall were smiling at Deepak when they saw him reading the same book.

"Why so many smiles?" asked Priya.

"My fans I believe!" said Deepak closing the book once for all.

"You must be really special then," said Priya trying to pull Deepak.

"She is talking finally," thought Deepak.

"Anyway what about the movie plan?" asked Deepak, "I almost became a sit-down comedian for that," he thought.

"We are going there now," Priya replied.

It was almost 2:00 PM and the Prasad at the temple was the only food that Deepak had eaten so far. Priya took him to a small theatre located at the outskirts of the city. Deepak kept thinking about all the various possible reasons for coming to a place like this.

"I have never been to this place before. Looks small but interesting," said Deepak.

"Yah it is an interesting place. This is one of the preferred spots for the city lovers who want to enjoy some slow paced romance!" said Priya.

"Really?" asked Deepak with a wide mouth.

"What are you excited about?" asked Priya puncturing all the energy that Deepak had gained in a second.

"Nothing, nothing, so what movie are we going to watch?" Deepak asked.

"That's a surprise. It's a movie you can't find anywhere in the city. We are going to watch the premier show of a special movie!"

"Something sounds interesting finally," Deepak thought.

On entering the theatre, Deepak realized it to be much smaller from the inside. There were hardly 100 seats in the theatre and most of the seats were occupied.

Once seated, Priya excused herself for a minute and left the place.

"Dude, going to watch movie with Priya all alone," Deepak texted to Aju

"What movie?"

"No clue. But it's a premier show and it's meant only for VIPs. I am feeling good about the movie already."

"Whatever, dude, come home with a beer case. We need to celebrate!"

"Why celebrate? Nothing good has happened between us so far."

"You've been telling me this for the past three months. What the hell are you doing? Are you her bodyguard or what?"

"Patience dude, patience. I want to take it slowly. Anyway, the beer case is confirmed, I am sort of having a triple date today."

"Great, three cases in that case," came the instant text from Aju.

"Go to sleep," replied Deepak and ended the texting session.

Priya came back wearing a different dress. It was black tee and jeans.

"Is this your movie watching costume?" asked Deepak with a smile.

"Yah, only for today," said Priya and quickly settled in her seat.

"Will you at least tell me now what movie are we going to watch?" asked Deepak with the least interest in the movie.

"Come on, you have come so far, can't you wait for some more time?"

"I guess I can," said Deepak and slowly glanced around at the people sitting in the hall. All of them were wearing the same black T-Shirt.

“What is happening? Everyone is wearing the same dress,” Deepak asked in surprise.

“Why are you so restless? Sit and enjoy the movie with the date you have brought,” said Priya with a funny accent.

“Sure, sure. It’s our date, I forgot,” said Deepak trying to build up the conversation. Meanwhile, the movie title flashed on the screen.

“Not my day in any stretch of imagination,” Deepak thought and settled back in his seat.

Once the movie credits began to roll, there was a huge applause from the crowd including from Priya. She was totally engrossed in the film that she even forgot that Deepak was with her.

It was the first scene of the movie and it was a racing circuit with cars lining up at the start line. Then the camera suddenly shifted to a deserted location where a brand new car which belonged to the Hero was burned down by a few villains. The Villains laugh at the Hero and throw ashes on his face. The camera shifts back to the racing circuit and there was no clue of the hero’s whereabouts.

The countdown starts for the race and by the time the clock becomes zero, the hero jumps into the circuit with his bullock cart with amazing speed. The whole theatre jumps up in joy, including Priya.

“Dude, I am not sure if my hangover is over or not. I am seeing things!” Deepak texted Aju.

“Believe me. The same thing happened to me now. I have cleared my economics paper. Can you believe it?” came the reply.

“I know I am dreaming now!” Deepak said to himself and continued watching the movie.

The Car vs Bullock Cart race continued for another 15 minutes when a train entered the circuit to hinder the Hero who was leading the race. Unperturbed by the obstacles, the Hero proceeded until he saw a puppy suddenly running towards the train. The hero jumped off his speeding cart and saved the puppy and got back on his cart to win the race. "Holy S@#t!" thought Deepak and was about to make a sarcastic remark about the movie when he saw Priya standing on top of her chair and shouting like a drunk cheerleader. Deepak decided to calm down as he thought the movie was better than Priya's cheering. He succumbed to his seat and began to watch the miserable movie. The movie continued to baffle Deepak in all possible ways. He was not sure how to react to every scene. The Hero, after all his heroism, enters Pakistan to find his lost girlfriend. After a lot of heroism again, he escapes from the country with his girlfriend. During the escape, he grabs his girlfriend's hand on a running train where he encounters another man who incidentally is the girl's Pakistani boyfriend. The Hero, amidst the entire struggle, gets them married in the train while the train crosses the Indo –Pakistan Border.

"Are you serious?" Deepak thought and looked at Priya again. This time she was jumping along with the other people in the theatre.

"Looks like everything happens for a reason. If not for the movie I would have never known about Priya's choices!" thought Deepak.

"Priya, shall we go now?' asked Deepak but Priya could not hear him amidst the loud crowd cheers.

"Dude, take my statement. This movie will go into History as the worst movie ever made!" texted Deepak.

"Who cares about a movie when a girl is beside him?" was the reply from Aju.

"What if the girl likes/loves the movie?" texted back Deepak

"Mmmm… that's interesting. Maybe the movie is not your type. So don't make a big fuss about it!"

"Fuss… Have you ever seen a movie where the hero races a bullock cart in an F1 circuit?"

"That's nice. He should be a superhero then. Won't you accept this if it was a Hollywood movie?"

"Go back to sleep, Dude!" texted Deepak in frustration.

"So did you enjoy the movie?" asked Priya stepping down from the chair.

"Yah, it was good. The storyline could have been better, but otherwise, everything was good!" answered Deepak.

Priya kept looking at Deepak for a while and said, "Who expects a storyline in a spoof movie?"

"Spoof?" thought Deepak but replied saying, "Yah that's true!"

"It's a spoof of most Indian movies. I thought that the response was amazing!" said Priya walking out of the theatre.

"Mmmm... Yeah, yeah. The response was awesome!" said Deepak without noticing the smile on Priya's face.

"You really don't have any clue about spoof movies, do you?" Priya asked.

Deepak gave a pitiful, bizarre and a nervous smile at Priya.

"Cho Chweet!" smiled Priya pinching Deepak's cheek.

"What the f@#$? " Deepak thought.

"She just pinched my cheek Dude. I feel like a kitty or something!" texted Deepak.

"Dude, come on. It's a sign of love. Don't text me now. Be with her and wait for the right time!"

"Right time for F#$%g what?" Deepak texted Aju, when Priya pulled him towards a tall fair guy.

"Deepak this is Siddharth and Sid this is Deepak," said Priya.

Deepak gave him an acknowledging smile whereas Sid was least bothered to reciprocate. Priya continued, "Sid is my childhood friend and incidentally the director of this blockbuster which you had just watched!"

"So did you like it?" asked Sid looking at Deepak.

"Yah, it was good and unique!" replied Deepak trying not to say anymore.

"I simply loved it, Sid. You have created magic out there. Fingers crossed for your theatrical release!" said Priya, all smiles.

"Thanks sweetie, just pray for me. Now excuse me people, I have an interview to attend to!" said Sid and left the spot in a jiffy.

"He will be famous soon!" said Priya, looking at Sid wistfully as he was rushing to the exit.

"I am sure he will!" Deepak said.

"By the way why didn't you give your honest feedback to him?" asked Priya.

"It was honest feedback, trust me!"

"Mmmm… I always feel that you try to please me rather speaking your mind."

"Nothing like that, Priya. I am a bit soft to disagree with people as I am sensitive to their sensitivity!"

"Mmmm... Whatever you say. So what are your plans for the rest of the day?" asked Priya looking at her watch.

"Nothing much, I have to get back to my long pending assignments!"

"You are so boring, Deepak!"

"I know. The assignments are still worse!" Deepak replied.

"Anyway, shall we leave then or do you have anything else to say?" asked Priya again.

"Say what?" asked Deepak and began to walk towards the exit.

It was a calm trip back to the college. Priya spent most of the journey speaking to her friends who were mostly boys which irritated Deepak to hell. He too wanted to show off and called Aju who was still in bed. Aju was least bothered to pick up the call, however this did not deter Deepak from pretending to speak to him.

After reaching college, Deepak bid Priya goodbye and walked towards the canteen. His eyes were wet. He felt that Priya couldn't understand him and his feelings for her. When he reached the canteen, he saw Aju sitting in a corner, sipping his black coffee.

"So, how was it?" asked Aju in a broken voice courtesy ice cold beer.

"Everything is over. She can never love me; she likes my sterile and safe company, that's it and nothing more!"

"Did you cry?" asked Aju looking at Deepak's red eyes.

"Don't ask me anything, just leave me alone for some time!" said Deepak.

Aju didn't anticipate Deepak would have so much in him. He slowly asked him, "Why don't you try Anshul? I think she has feelings for you!"

Deepak gave him a hard look, which made Aju empty his coffee mug in jiffy and run away.

Deepak closed his eyes and rested his head on the table. His most anticipated day had come to a disastrous end. Deepak's day started with the thought of Priya and ended with it. He thought everything was over and he needed a new motivation to finish the rest of the days at the college. He kept on thinking and slowly slept off.

"Do you need a beer?" A sharp voice asked.

Deepak woke up to the voice and found Priya sitting in front of him.

"I know you hate early mornings but you still make it to the morning group sessions. I know you hate economics but still your electives include economics. I know you hate going to temples but you still make it to the Friday evening pujas. I know you hate missing parties but you still attend the social awareness events at college. I knew you did all of this just to be closer to me!" said Priya. "I can still add more to this list but all I wanted to ask was that if you can do all of these which you generally don't then why not this?"

"Which one?" Deepak asked with a blank face.

"Expressing your love to me."

"You knew it?" Deepak was dumbstruck.

"Not just me, even the priest at the temple did," giggled Priya.

Deepak after a long thought asked, "Did you set him up?"

"Not just him!" smiled Priya and started to move out.

"But, but... "

"What but but?" asked Priya as she continued to walk away.

"But you said…"

"What "I said"? I said nothing!"

"No no, not that, about me saying..."

"Say what?"

"That thing Priya!"

"Final Chance, Deepak!" Priya said without even looking at him.

"I Love You, I Love You, I Love You!" shouted Deepak at the peak of his voice and this time the entire crowd at the canteen was cheering him on.

Priya turned around with a pleasant smile and said, "Finally!"

Two Years Ago

It was Priya's birthday and Deepak wanted to celebrate it differently at the beach. As per the plan, Priya reached the beach at 6:00 PM but she could not find Deepak. She tried calling him but he wasn't picking up the call. Priya assumed that Deepak must have been driving down to the beach. After half-an-hour, Priya received a message from Deepak saying, "Sorry Sweetheart, stuck in this stupid meeting and the Boss is in a shitty mood. I'll rush there once the meeting finishes. Please go to our regular restaurant and wait there, I will reach in another 15 - 20 minutes!"

Priya was furious but she knew that she had no other choice but to wait. The evening started to get darker and Priya was not comfortable standing alone on the beach. She took a cab and went to the restaurant. On reaching the restaurant, Priya felt the atmosphere to be far more different than it used to be. She felt that everyone was looking at her strangely. She ignored their looks and decided to wait. After a couple of minutes, she decided to use the washroom. When she walked out, she sensed someone was standing behind her. Priya panicked and started to move fast when a stranger stopped her from the front pointing a pistol on her head.

Priya went numb and started to sweat.

"Just do it as we say and stay alive!" said the stranger. Priya shook her head without resistance as she was in a state of shock. Her mind started to imagine fearful things. "Please leave me, I will give you everything I have with me, just let me go!"Priya began to plead.

There was no reply from the kidnappers as their mind was already engrossed with the exit plans. The two kidnappers slowly took Priya through the restaurant hall with the revolver directed at her back. Nobody at the restaurant took a second look at Priya which made her suspicious about the people at the restaurant.

The kidnappers took Priya and entered the cab which was waiting for them at the entrance. Priya was blindfolded and was taken far away from the city. She continued pleading but the kidnappers hardly bothered. With every passing minute, Priya got restless with fear. After an hour's ride, the vehicle came to a halt. The kidnappers tried to pull Priya out from the cab but she tried to resist the pull but their force was too hard to fight. The kidnappers literally dragged Priya out of the cab and made her walk through sand and finally pushed her into a boat.

"Where are you taking me?" Priya cried with her blindfold on.

Once on the boat, she was taken into a small room and was tied to a chair. The Kidnappers left the room slamming the door with a heavy thud.

Priya's heart beat heavily. She wished that somebody at the restaurant would inform Deepak when he reached. She began to think about the recent incidents of rape and murder and started to panic. She made up her mind to run away from the place once she got a chance, but the realization that she was on a boat scared her. She kept praying to God and wished that a miracle happened.

"Mike check! Mike check!" a voice came from a speaker nearby.

Priya found the voice to be too familiar.

The voice continued.

"My life was in total darkness until you embraced it like a rainbow. My life was more of a ritual until you infused heaven into it!"

"Deepak!" Priya shouted, "Is that you?"

The voice continued.

"Before falling in love with you nobody took me seriously including me but after you came, even I have started to know me. I suddenly felt a purpose in my life and started to live the day interestingly just to tell you tales in the evening. I added details to my life and subtracted the boredom. The beeps of your messages and the pings of your chat added spark to my heartbeat. Negativity did not matter anymore to me as my little life could accommodate only your thoughts and love!"

Priya sat still listening to the talk and her eyes were moist again, this time out of happiness.

The voice continued.

"You were the first to admire my unshaven face and the first to pull out my grey hair. I would have never thought of dancing on stage if you were not one in the audience. My public life became private, reserved just for you. I started seeing the power in my words when you gave all your attention and time to it. Some say LOVE is Loss of Valuable Energy but for me your LOVE is the source of my energy. When you are with me, the world is my playground and my life is a play. With you in my team, victory can only be mine. Thank God you are born in this world and thank God I am born again because of you. So it's not just your birthday but also my rebirth day. Happy Birthday, Sweetheart. Let God give me all the power to make you live like an angel. Sweet Heart, thank you for being there for me, Happy Birthday again!"

Priya's eyes flowed with tears, she forgot all that happened to her before this and forgave Deepak for the prank he had played on her. She pushed herself out from the chair and fell flat on the floor. Her hands were not tied and the rope was left loose. Priya removed her blindfold and rushed out of the room.

When she came out of the room, her sight fell on the calm sea which was glowing bright under the full moonlight. She walked forward and was blown away by the magnificent decorations on the boat. The whole boat was decorated with lights and flowers! It was like a little dream in the middle of the sea. Priya never felt so special and looked around for Deepak. She spotted him standing at the fore end of the boat. She ran towards him with tears blurring her vision and gave him the tightest hug of her life.

Kissing Deepak on his cheek, she asked, "Why did you come into my life so late?"

A year ago

It was their first night after the wedding. As per custom, Deepak was first sent into a colorful bedroom and was asked to wait for Priya with a glass of milk.

Once inside the room, Deepak had other plans, he wanted to play a prank. He locked the door and undressed himself. He opened his bag and took out a silk sari along with the requisite accessories. He started wearing it along with some heavy makeup, courtesy the makeup kits of Priya. Deepak wore the long wig which he had rented at a bargain price. Once satisfied with his look, which, according to him, was flashy and glowing, he unlocked the door without opening it and stood at a distance expecting Priya to enter.

He waited for a while, but there was no sign of Priya. During the wait, Deepak decided to add a little spark to his looks. He picked up a small ring from Priya's dressing table and tried to fix it on his belly button. Meanwhile, Priya's father, Rao realized that the Air conditioner remote was misplaced in the hall. He decided to hand it over to Deepak before their big night. Without a warning, he picked the remote and walked towards the first night room and opened the door. Rao stood at the entrance, stunned. Never in his life was he this stunned. He could neither speak nor move from his position.

Deepak on the other side with the ring hanging from his belly button, gave him the most confused smile of his life. He could hardly speak, either. With all the courage left in him, he said, "Looks like my belly button is too deep!"

Rao placed the remote on the floor and moved out like a robot. Deepak was embarrassed and was not sure why he said what he had said. He was pissed; he removed his sari and threw it on the floor with disgust. Priya, who was carrying the milk, saw her father speaking to himself in solitude. She approached him and asked him, "Are you alright dad?"

Rao looked at her and asked, "Are you sure he is a software guy?"

"Dad, He is not only the software guy but also the softest guy I have ever seen!" Priya said with a wink. "But why this question now?" asked Priya again.

"Nothing, he looks more like a fashion designer to me!"

"Mmmm... With his dressing sense he is no less than a fashion designer too!" Priya said trying to heighten Deepak's image in her father's mind.

"Whatever!" said Rao and walked away.

Priya was a little confused over her father's remarks. She walked to the bedroom and opened the door. She saw Deepak in a blouse and in-skirt with the sari thrown across the room. With this costume, he sat on the bed, indulging in jalebis. This time it was Priya's turn to get stunned. However, she rushed inside the room and closed the door before anybody could take a peek.

"Deepak, Deepak!" she called twice making sure that it was Deepak. With a mouthful of Jalebis, Deepak turned towards Priya and said "Surprise!" Priya sat down on the floor more shocked than surprised.

With a low volume she asked, "Please tell me that this is just a prank and you are not different!"

Controlling his laughter, Deepak said, "How does it matter, the damage is done. You are my wife now!"

Realizing it to be a prank, she jumped on Deepak with a rage and gave the first night bumps with all her strength. This fight eventually turned out to be too intimate to be fought with the clothes on and their fight turned out into amazing love.

Holding Priya in his arms, Deepak asked, "So how did you find my prank?"

"Disgusting, now I realize how shocked my Dad would have been seeing you in a sari!"

"I don't think he was shocked, I believe he was checking me out!"

"Stupid!" answered Priya with a slow smile.

"And how was your first night romance?" asked Deepak with a twinkle in his eyes.

"I felt like a lesbian tonight and believe me it was not that bad!"

"Oh, really?" said Deepak and started tickling Priya ending their memorable first night.

***

After a dramatic first night, Deepak woke up late in the morning to find Priya missing from bed. He got out of the room and found Priya's father reading the newspaper in the verandah.

Noticing Deepak out of the room, he said, "Oh, you woke up finally, please come sit and have a cup of tea!"

Deepak, without any reluctance, sat in front of him and started making his tea.

"So, finally married?" asked Rao with a smile.

"Yah, it is yet to sink in though!" replied Deepak.

"Don't worry, it will sink when you start sinking in with responsibilities!"

"Yah, true!" said Deepak, trying to smile artificially.

"So, Deepak tell me how much do you earn per month?"

"Sufficient enough to keep Priya happy, Sir!" answered Deepak with a little annoyance.

"That you need not bother Deepak, she is earning well for herself and I suppose it's better than your pay," said Rao.

"Sir, sorry for changing the topic but this tea sucks, let me find myself some coffee." Deepak walked away from the conversation and went to the terrace, trying to calm himself.

"Are you alright?" asked Priya who was following him to the terrace.

"Yah, why are you asking?" asked Deepak.

"Just like that. So you like my home and my parents?"

"Yah, your parents are great and so is your house. I can understand how much they love you!"

"That's something special for all single children. They never said no to me, ever. Even for our marriage, they hardly showed any resistance."

Deepak listened to Priya and decided not to discuss anything negative about her parents with her. "So, Priya tell me when are we going to our house?" Deepak asked.

"You mean your house?" Priya asked without giving it a thought.

"Well, my house is now our house, right?"

"Yah, it is, But Deepak these are my last few days at my house, so will you mind if we stay here for a bit longer?"

"How long?"

"Maybe a month's time, only if it is okay with you!"

Deepak did not want to disappoint Priya though he knew he had to face her father for the next 30 days. He also knew that his mother would not like this idea but still he did not want to disappoint Priya.

"As you wish, my princess!" smiled Deepak.

The next 29 days were the longest in Deepak's life, with his father-in-Law's irritation on one hand, and office pressure on the other. Deepak's company was downsizing and this was putting too much pressure on him to safeguard his job. To add to this annoyance there was his mother's call every now and then asking when he would come home. He had to hide all this and present a happy face to Priya all the time. The fear of losing his job made Deepak lose sleep, he began to find solace in smoking and alcohol. He made sure that Priya didn't suspect him whenever he returned home.

6 months ago

Now, it was Priya's turn to cope with her in-laws. There was hardly anything common between her and Deepak's mother. She tried hard to conceal all the differences within. However, there were many instances where she could not stop complaining to Deepak about his mother. Deepak's mother on the other hand, was too possessive about Deepak, and she could not tolerate a new girl taking control over him within such a short span of time. She kept telling Deepak about all the difficulties she had faced in raising him as a single mother.

As if this was not enough, Deepak's younger sister, Usha came to her mother's place to spend the summer vacation with her two sons. Priya tried to get friendly with Usha, but Usha didn't reciprocate. She was jealous of Priya for her job and her looks. She joined hands with her mom and enjoyed cursing Priya. Her two sons were so naughty that Priya avoided speaking to them. Once, Usha's younger son, while playing with Priya's phone, dropped it on the floor and broke it into pieces. Priya was furious and shouted at him. This led to a clash between Usha and Priya and eventually, Deepak's mom took Usha's side. Frustrated with all of this, Priya left the house in tears.

Priya called Deepak and asked him to meet her immediately at their regular coffee shop. Deepak was too busy at office, he had to make a presentation to the most important client of his company and he was already running short of time. Priya refused to accept any excuse and asked him to meet him immediately or else she would never go back to his home. After hearing this, Deepak could not concentrate on his work either; he stopped work abruptly and rushed to meet Priya without intimating his colleagues. When he met Priya, she sat at the centre of the coffee house and sobbed uncontrollably.

"What are you doing? Please stop crying. Everyone is looking at you!" pleaded Deepak.

"Stop instructing me. You better control your sister and your mother!"

Deepak got annoyed when he heard Priya complaining about his mother.

"Now what? You want me to shout at them and make them feel guilty?" he asked controlling his temper.

Priya remained calm. She shot Deepak a dirty look and walked out of the coffee shop without saying a word.

Deepak sat there in total despair. He tried to call Priya but she did not answer his call. Next, he called her mother but she did not pick up either. Frustrated with this, he decided to go back home and take control over the situation. When he reached home, he noticed that Usha had already left the house with her two kids. Deepak's mother was inconsolable; she cursed Priya repeatedly about her attitude. Deepak could not tolerate this either, however, he could not raise his voice and calmly left for his office. When he reached his office, he saw his colleagues looking at him in a bizarre way. He was ordered to meet the boss immediately.

On reaching the Boss' office, he pleaded, "Sorry, Sir, some family issues and I could not avoid them!"

The boss, without looking at Deepak, said, "Please don't make me speak more. You have been here for so long and you know what the company is going through. During these times of recession, all that the company needs is a small mistake to sack people and today we almost lost our top client because of you. You have literally printed your own pink slip. Go solve all your family problems and begin afresh somewhere."

Deepak was shattered. All that he had done for this company had disappeared just like that. There was not a single soul to support him as they had to hold onto their dear jobs. Deepak walked out of the once lively campus with no one beside him.

"Life sucks, Dude, want to die!" Deepak said to Aju via text.

"Same here, we'll better die drinking. In our regular bar in one hour!" came back the reply.

❋❋❋

"So what exactly is your problem? Is it your wife, or your mother or your job?" asked Aju, opening his third can of beer.

"All the above with some more missing in the list!"

"Chill dude. Give things time, everything will be alright."

"Anyway. I don't want any advice. All I need is your apartment to stay for a while till things settle down." said Deepak.

"What do you mean by settle down? It is not a riot, it is your family, only you have to settle it."

"Now you better stop your bull shit and just drink your beer!" said Deepak who was getting high with alcohol and anger. Deepak's phone rang. It was Priya calling.

"She doesn't answer my calls! How the fuck does she expect me to pick up her calls?" asked Deepak and disconnected the call.

The phone rang again and it was Priya again. Deepak disconnected it again.

This continued for some more time and Deepak was furious. He smashed his phone on the ground in rage and screamed. Ajay tried to pacify him but he could not succeed as Deepak was drunk beyond all limits. He was pushed out of the bar by the bouncers. Aju, despite being drunk as well, took Deepak home. The house was locked and there was a note taped to the door.

It said, "Mother is not well. Taking her to Rishi Hospital!"

Priya had written the note in a hurry. Deepak panicked and all his intoxication disappeared in a second. He rushed to the hospital. As he was about to enter the hospital, he saw Priya and a whole lot of his relatives coming out. Priya was crying inconsolably.

Holding Priya's hands Deepak asked. "What happened?"

"She had a major cardiac arrest."

"Why didn't you call me?" shouted Deepak.

Wiping her tears, she said, "Not a word more, Deepak!" she paused and with a broken voice, said, "She kept asking for you till the last moment!"

Deepak refused to speak to anybody for the next two days. He kept cursing himself for his mother's death and wished that he was with her for just one extra day. After the funeral, when Deepak returned home, he felt a deep vacuum within himself. He could not control his tears and began to cry like a baby. When Priya came to console him, Usha pushed her away from him.

"You are responsible for my mother's death. Don't you dare take my brother also!" she shouted.

Unable to tolerate this comment, Priya got wild and slapped Usha hard on her face.

"Get out of this house!" Priya shouted at Usha.

"No, you are out of this house. It's because of you that my mother's health was spoiled and now you are slapping my sister in front of me! I don't want to see your fucking face anymore, leave now and never return!" shouted Deepak at Priya.

Saying these words Deepak left the house. After four hours, he returned, fully intoxicated. He slowly moved around the house and as expected Priya was not there. He saw his phone which he had smashed at the bar, repaired and placed on the centre table. A small note was attached to it and it said, "Don't call me ever - Ajay."

Now, what wrong did I do to him? Deepak thought. This was the beginning of his solitude for the days to come. Days turned into weeks and weeks into months but Deepak was yet to regain control over his life. He became addicted to alcohol. His day started and ended with alcohol and occasional drugs became a routine. He stopped picking up calls and eventually he stopped receiving calls including those from Priya. Solitude killed him more than the alcohol did. He didn't know what to do and kept worrying about all that had happened. This was when he received a message from Ajay.

"Are you still alive?" Deepak would not have bothered to reply to the message a month ago, but today, he was alone and needed company even if it was just through an SMS.

"Yah, but not sure for how long," Deepak replied.

"Why? What happened?"

"Why do you bother?"

"Because I am Aju and I know you more than you know yourself."

"Stop the bullshit. You didn't even call me and even now you are only texting!"

"That's because I can't speak. Please don't ask me anything more about this if you want our chat to continue!"

Deepak paused for a second. A lot of thoughts filled his mind. He decided not to ask anything about it for the moment.

"I miss you dude. I miss u badly!" texted Deepak after a while

"I miss you too. Are you drunk?"

"What do you think? Always!"

"Are you alone?"

"All the time!"

"What about mom and Priya?"

"Mother left the world and Priya left me."

"If it's a joke, stop right there. I am in no mood for it!"

"No mood for jokes? My life is a big joke here!" Deepak typed, with a heavy heart.

There was no message from Ajay for a while. Then, a long one came in.

"There was a pet dog which was taken care by a beautiful family, but the dog always had the impulse to escape away and enjoy freedom. On one such day, the dog was taken for a walk and it escaped from the owner's clutches. It ran miles and miles away from home. It loved the freedom for a while but when it realized it needed food, it was lost. It kept wandering for food but it could not find a single soul to offer food. It didn't feel special anymore. Stray dogs started chasing it and it had to keep on running with an empty stomach. It started searching for food in the garbage and that was when it found a dry bone. The dog grabbed it and started running; it went to a hiding spot and started to relish the bone. The bone was dry and sharp and it started piercing the dog's mouth and blood started to ooze. Meanwhile, an old dog which was passing by, saw the blood from the dog's mouth and warned the dog about the blood. The dog thought that the old dog was jealous of its food and ignored its threat. It continued to bite the bone not realizing that it was tasting its own blood."

Deepak read the message but he did not reply.

"You have already run too far but you are still not lost. Your addiction is the bone and you are tasting your own blood!" Ajay wrote.

With no more messages from Ajay, Deepak was left with the memory of the dog story which kept haunting him for the rest of the day. With an intoxicated mind, his fear of losing life increased and he realized that he needed to start somewhere before it was too late. He woke up late the next morning and the first thing he did was to skip the morning drink. This was not easy. Alcohol had become more of a company to him rather than an addiction. He wanted to put an end to this solitude and decided to meet his friends and family. He did not consider calling Priya who was staying alone in her company flat. Priya, on the other hand, was clueless about her future with Deepak and was waiting for his call since the time she left his house.

Deepak invited some of his close friends for a little chat but none of them obliged as they were either reluctant or busy. Then, he called Usha for a chat, but the call went unanswered. At the end of the day, Deepak felt worse than he did the day before and could not stop himself from picking up the whiskey bottle again.

He texted Ajay, "I want to meet you Ajay. I am living in hell here and I think I am getting into depression."

"That's not possible Deepak; my present condition won't allow me to meet anybody, but thankfully I am open to texting."

"What the fuck is your problem Aju? Why don't you tell me? I will help you no matter what, believe me!"

"Help yourself first, I am perfectly alright except that I can't meet you or speak to you. Please don't start on this topic again for God's sake!"

"Whatever man, I won't bother you anymore and no fucking SMS anymore!" texted Deepak.

With increasing intoxication, Deepak's anger for Ajay began to recede. He knew that he was the one whom he can trust at the end of the day. He texted Aju again, saying, "Sorry dude, I was not myself. This solitude gets deadlier with every passing day. Sometimes I wonder how ambitious I was and how all of a sudden life became a big zero. The more I try to come out of it, the deeper it becomes!"

"I understand your condition man. I was in a similar state for sometime after college. No job and more dreams is a deadly combination. This too shall pass!"

"Mmmm…"

"What mmmm..?"

"Nothing Ajay, I never even dreamt that life could take such a vicious turn for me!"

"Why not? When it happens to everybody it can happen to you as well!"

"But what wrong did I do? All I wanted in life was to be good!"

"What good are you talking about?"

"Being a good son, a good husband, a good friend, a good worker and a good person in society. Tell me, what is wrong with it?"

"Well, on the whole nothing is wrong with your thought, but on a deeper level, there is a logical problem with this thought."

"What Logical Problem? Seriously dude, you sound like the same old college Ajay!"

"Logic says that you can't be everything at the same time. Either be a good husband and reach home on time or be a good worker and work late at office. Either be a good son spending more time with your parents or be a good parent spending more time with your children."

"This sounds stupid. It looks as if I can be good to only one person!"

"True, you can be good to only one person at a time. You prioritize the person based on the time and never try to be good to everybody every time, that's a recipe for disaster!"

"Man, you sound different now. Are you into some spirituality thing or something?"

"Stop judging me and start analyzing you. Got to leave now, will text you later, TC!"

Aju's last text started a long silence again for Deepak. He was left with no other option but to reiterate every word he read. The more he thought of it, the more sense it made to him.

Then there was a message from Aju, "It's the time for you to be the best husband dude, be that now or lose it forever."

Thanks to the intoxication, the thought of losing it forever terrified Deepak. He decided to meet Priya. He took his phone and searched for the address which Priya had texted him a long time ago.

❋❋❋

Deepak stood at the gate, confirming Priya's address with the watchman, when he noticed a familiar face driving out of the apartments. He tried hard to remember but he could not recollect.

With no further thought, he walked towards Priya's residence. He pressed the bell and there was no reply. He pressed it again and then came Priya's voice from inside, "Sid, is that you? Wait for a second, I am dressing up!"

The name Sid rang the bell in Deepak's mind. It was Sid whom he had seen driving out of the gates. A lot of thoughts rushed through his mind and he felt a sense of fire rising within. He felt like banging down the door and asking Priya what Sid would be doing there. But he tried to control his temper and just pass the moment. Priya opened the door and saw Deepak standing at the door with a dull and unshaven face, wearing dirty clothes. Priya could not believe what she was seeing. She walked back, sat on the sofa and cried uncontrollably. Deepak approached her and tried to pacify her.

"What happened to you, you did not bother to call me even. What wrong did I do to deserve this? I have been waiting for you all the while!"

"Sorry Priya, I wasn't me. I needed some time to recover."

"Then what about me? Where can I go?"

"Sorry again, let's put the past aside and start anew!" said Deepak looking at the longing face of Priya.

"Look at you. How long you've been drinking! Do you eat at all? God, I should have come and seen you!"

"No, I am okay now!"

"What okay, stupid? You look like a skeleton! Did you eat anything today?"

"Yah some chips and nuts," answered Deepak

Priya looked at him angrily and walked into the kitchen. With newfound happiness and vigour, Priya decided to make a quick snack for Deepak. Deepak on the other hand succumbed to the fresh ambience of Priya's residence and rested on the sofa. He began to relieve himself of all tension and looked around the cute little space which reflected Priya's perspectives. He browsed through the fashion magazines on the table and that was when he noticed a colorful card inserted in one of them.

It said, "The past is the past! Let's make a new beginning. My Love for you is still bigger now!"

Deepak quickly moved to the bottom of the card, it said "Yours- Only Yours – SID!"

The few seconds of calmness now rebounded into a fire of anger. "How can she do this to me!" he thought. He read and reread the card only to get his temper worse. Deepak could not control himself anymore, he looked around and found Priya's mobile on the top of the desk. Unable to control his suspicion, he took her phone and looked into the call history. All the recent calls in the phone were from Sid. Deepak was furious. He woke up and left the house smashing the door behind him. Ignorant of all the happenings, Priya was busy working in the kitchen.

"She is cheating on me Ajay. How could she do this to me?" Deepak texted sitting at the bar.

"How do you know that?" was the reply.

"Please stop interrogating me man, I am in no mood."

"Wait a second, are you at our bar?"

"Aju, you must know what Priya means to me dude!"

"I do, idiot, but I also know what you meant to her!"

"For God's sake stop that. She has found someone who is more successful and more handsome than I am!"

"Is that what you think?"

"Not think, I know!"

"Stop overreacting Deepak, stop."

Deepak stopped replying. He was engulfed by this sorrow with the liquor being a catalyst. He drank till he lost consciousness. All that was left on his mind was Priya's face.

Deepak's phone rang and it was Priya calling. He answered in rage and shouted, "I am done with you, Priya! If you love Sid, go ahead and live with him. There is no point adjusting with me. Please stop acting, I know every Fu##$% thing! I am too tired of you, stop calling me once for all and let me die in peace!"

He hung up. With the anger engulfing him, Deepak walked towards the bridge with his vulnerable intoxication.

"Are you there?" Aju texted.

Deepak saw the message on impulse and did not respond. "He can't even call his dying friend!" shouted Deepak at the top of his voice.

Deepak proceeded towards the bridge wall which once served as his secret smoking spot. Looking down from the bridge, he gasped. He closed his eyes and listened to his heart thumping. He paused for a second and with little thought, he decided to text Aju one last time before taking the plunge.

"Tell Priya that I loved her to death and she will be my first love forever, no matter what. Know what Aju? Our secret smoking spot will witness my last breath!"

Sending his message, Deepak composed himself to finish it once and for all when his phone beeped once more. Deepak wasn't sure if he had to look at it, but something told him to check it for one last time.

The text read: ""The same cigarettes have cursed me with cancer."

Deepak went blank, he kept staring at the text for long and it occurred to him why Ajay was reluctant to speak to him, because he could not. "Why didn't you tell me, Ass? How? When? Where are you? I want to see you now!"

"Please don't. You better die than seeing me!"

"Stupid, stop this nonsense. Where are you?"

"At the hospital, visit me tomorrow."

"Which hospital?"

"Can you do one final favor for me?"

"Which hospital?"

"Favour first."

"What the fuck do you want?"

"Visit that bastard SID and punch his face for me!"

"Seriously? Why are you bothered?"

"Because I had wasted my college days hitching you and Priya together and this Bastard Sid can't break it just like that!"

"Come on Aju, even I had given up on that!"

"I am shit concerned about you, it's about me. So will you do it or not?"

"I will do it if that's what you want, but for the record, it's not going to do me any good!"

"Again, it's not about you, ass hole. It's about me. So get your tummy tucked and go fucking do my job!"

Deepak stood still at the top of the bridge. He was confused like never before. Two minutes ago, he had made up his mind for the ultimatum and now, he had to stop everything for his sick friend. The rage he had for Priya suddenly disappeared. All that was running in his mind was Ajay and his disease. He wanted to ignore Aju's request to punch Sid but he knew that Aju would not give in until he got proof of Deepak having hit Sid. Deepak was left with no other choice but to go back to Priya's place to get Sid's address.

❁❁❁

Deepak stood at the doorstep, unable to decide if he should press the bell or not. The door opened and Sid stood at the door step. Deepak's dormant anger peaked again. Without wasting any time, he threw a punch on Sid's face with a fragile force. Sid retaliated with a blow in return, which brought Deepak down on the floor with blood oozing out of his nose. The next thing Deepak knew was that he was lying on the couch with cotton on his nostrils.

"What were you thinking?" asked Sid with piercing eyes.

"Take Priya and leave! But remember, one day, she will ditch you as well!" shouted Deepak.

"What are you talking about? Priya loved you like mad and you drunkard, you are blaming her!"

"And that's why you came to give her solace, right?" Deepak asked with a sarcastic smile.

"Are you hinting at something? If you think something is between us than listen carefully. Priya is a caring soul and I had sought her support more than she had sought mine. Today, if I am standing in front of you with my wife, it is because of all the efforts she put in. Despite all the hardship you have put her through, there was hardly an instance when she spoke ill of you. But look at you! How easily you doubt her character. You don't deserve her!" said Sid.

Sid called her wife who was standing in the kitchen waiting for the fight to be settled. Deepak noticed a young lady coming out of the kitchen holding a greeting card which Deepak had noticed before among Priya's magazines. Things were getting clearer, despite the blurred vision.

"But where is Priya?" Deepak asked in a pitiful voice.

Sid hardly bothered to reply. He left the room with his wife. There was nobody but silence to accompany Deepak. Sid's words kept echoing in Deepak's ears and thanks to the alcohol, again, the guilty feeling made him feel like dying again. After a brief pause, Sid's wife entered the room and said, "Priya was speaking to somebody on phone and after that she left the room without saying a word. She looked very upset." In an instant, Deepak knew that the call she was referring to was the one where he shouted at Priya sometime ago.

❋❋❋

Priya's phone was switched off. It did not deter Deepak from calling her 25 times in the past 20 minutes. He was not sure where to look for her. He tried calling Priya's parents but their phones were switched off, too. Out of sheer desperation, he took a cab and went to Priya's parents' place. He found that her parents were on a foreign trip. Deepak ran out of choices. He went back to Priya's flat to check if she had returned but her flat was empty. He checked the kitchen only to find his favorite mushroom and peas, beautifully decorated and left on a plate. The peas were assembled in the shape of a heart. Deepak could not control his tears. "What have I done?" he shouted. Sadness, guilt and anger made him weak and desperate.

Deepak's mind started to go haywire. "What if she decides to do something bad?" he asked himself.

He wrote a note and left it on the table before running back to the roads in search of his love. The note said, "Priya, I don't even qualify for an apology but trust me that's all that I have. I don't know why I became like this. My love for you was the only thing I was sure about, but today, by doubting you, I have failed even in that. My ego had spoiled me and now it's killing me. Some minutes ago, I wanted to kill myself. But now, I want to live. I will spend this remaining life saying sorry to you even if you forgive me. I don't know if you will ever read this. I am afraid, Priya. Maybe it's the alcohol in me speaking, or maybe not. But I am terrified. I don't want to lose you. You mean everything to me and please don't do anything stupid for this mistake of mine. Even if you detest me I will be there for you forever!"

The letters on the note were in a moist blue.

The night was a living hell for Deepak. He wandered around the city looking for Priya. He went to the Railway Station, the Bus Stations, malls, the beach and even registered a missing person's complaint at the police station. He didn't sense the blood dripping from his injured nose onto his mouth and then onto his white shirt. As the night got darker, his mind grew blank and he started wandering around aimlessly, forgetting what he was looking for. The night got tired as well and went to rest. With red eyes, a red shirt and a red mouth, Deepak sat down by the beach, looking at the rising sun. His phone beeped. With a sudden gush of life he read the text.

"Are you alive?" Aju messaged.

Sad that it was not from Priya, Deepak replied saying, "Like Never Before."

"Happy to hear that man, so are things sorted out?"

"Almost. You tell me. How is your health?" Deepak wrote back, trying to change the subject.

"Not yet sorted, then? Listen, dude I know you and Priya. You both love each other like mad. The only thing missing in your relationship is the star on top!" Aju wrote.

"Star?"

"Star indicating no conditions apply. Love her unconditionally with no expectations in return. You will be happy no matter what. I mean no matter what!"

"Who are you man? You speak like a saint!"

"Courtesy- Cancer. Anyway. Is Priya with you now?"

"I don't know where she is. I am getting furious, Aju. I am afraid she might do something stupid!"

"Stop fearing and give things time to settle, everything will be alright!"

Deepak found a comfort in Aju's texts, superseding the fear that was residing in him.

“So what should I do now?” asked Deepak.

“Go home, get some sleep and I am serious about it!”

Deepak rose with the sun and walked towards the beachside tea stall. Sipping his tea, he decided to visit Priya’s flat one more time before returning home.

❁❁❁

He walked into the open doors of Priya’s flat. Things were the same as last night. Deepak glanced at Priya’s stuff and got emotional with thoughts of her all over his mind. He continued to walk till he reached the kitchen. The mushroom and peas were still there, but with ants and flies on it. Deepak grabbed the plate and ate the stale dish with extra salt through his tears. He lay on Priya’s bed for some time, before leaving the place. With a heavy heart he closed the door and walked out.

“Maybe that’s it. She is not coming back to me!” he said to himself.

He decided to go back home with all reluctance. He knew that things were going to be bad again. He knew that he would get back to alcohol and smoking again, to escape reality and enter a world of illusions. Deepak opened the screeching gates and reached the door. As always, he had left his doors open. He moved in with heavy legs and sat on the bench, and kept his head down. As he was about to remove his sandal straps, he noticed a lovely pair of slippers lying there. Deepak kept trying to remove the strap but his hands kept shivering. Tears started to fall on his sandals. Deepak entered the living room and saw Priya sitting on the sofa with onions and mushrooms on a plate on the table. Realizing that Deepak had come, she tried to ignore him and kept looking at the muted television screen.

There was silence all around. Not expecting this much silence from Deepak, Priya turned around. She noticed that Deepak was on his knees with his hands folded.

"Forgive me; please forgive me!" he said in a broken voice.

Priya did not answer and was trying hard to hold back her tears but she could not. "Do you really love me?" she finally cried out. "You came to see me after such a long time, and that was what you thought of me?" she asked, crying. "I don't know where I had gone wrong Deepak, but I am really sorry for all that I had done to you!" she cried inconsolably.

"No Priya! Please don't cry! You did not do anything wrong. All of this is my fault. The only mistake you made was to love a stupid man like me!" said Deepak, crying.

Wiping his eyes Deepak said, "You know what? I have been crying too much of late. I think there is some hormone imbalance in me!"

Priya smiled.

"Will you forgive me?" asked Deepak with a sense of longing. She did not reply. She hugged Deepak with all her love. It was the best hug of their lives and they did not want to get out from it for a long time.

Holding her, Deepak said, "All this while, I have been thinking only about me but it was only yesterday I realized that there was no me without you!"

Priya had happy tears. "I am sorry for taking you for granted!"

Deepak smiled and asked, "So will you stop fighting with me, then?"

"No, not at all, it will only get bigger this time!" smiled Priya as they kissed.

❁❁❁

Munching on fresh Mushrooms, Deepak texted Aju. "Thank you Aju, you gave me my life back. Now I can fight with her every day! ☺ I am coming to meet you today."

"You are welcome, dude. By the way, don't try to meet me."

"Why not?"

"Because I am not your Aju."

"What?"

"I have stored Aju's number as the office number in your phone so you will neither call nor answer that number. I have even blacklisted the number to prevent incoming calls and messages."

Deepak was stunned. He was not able to react. "Is this a dream?" he thought and pinched himself. It wasn't.

"Who are you? How did you change the number in my cell phone?" Deepak asked, texting rapidly.

"Now that you are not drunk, give it a thought, you shall get the answer," came the reply.

Not trying to think too much about the phone thing, Deepak texted again. "Can we meet?"

"Let's see. I will invite you someday."

"But who are you?" texted Deepak again unable to control his curiosity.

There was no reply. Deepak called the number but the phone was switched off.

Not Today

Vivi could not concentrate on his morning paper despite it being his favorite part of the day. Drinking his tea, he tried to concentrate on the business column. But, the words on the paper meant nothing to his wavering mind. He moved on to his favorite sports column to check out the previous day's tennis results. After spending some time on it, he finished his tea thinking about his problem. He began rehearsing ways to ask leave for his much awaited family vacation. Every time he came up with a suitable request, he got skeptical about his boss' likely responses. With time running out, he decided to rehearse the rest of it at office. He had a quick shower and got dressed up in no time. He skipped his breakfast and gave no attention to his annoyed wife. He kissed his four-year-old son goodbye and rode his bike to work.

Racing amidst the peak traffic, Vivi almost dashed against a passing truck. Without bothering, he continued to maneuver his bike to office. He was the first to be at the office door, which was yet to be opened. Sensing comfort at his extra punctuality, he began to wait for the security to open the door. Vivi believed that by reaching office well before everyone, he would impress his superiors. To achieve this, he had to skip his breakfast and family time on all working days. Unable to wait anymore for the security guard, he sat on the stairs and opened his laptop. Vivi knew that his company's regional conference was expected to take place in a week's time and that he had to start working on the presentation for it. With the family vacation on the one hand and the company's presentation on the other, he knew that he had to suffer if he missed out on either. He continued working for some time when the company's security guard reached.

"Good Morning, Sir!" greeted the security guard.

"Coming late has become a norm for you nowadays! Stop this immediately or else I have to issue your firing order," said Vivi in a commanding voice.

"Sorry sir, I had to take my wife to hospital again," the guard replied.

"You better stop giving all these lame excuses. Now quickly open the doors and switch on all the lights and ACs!" said Vivi closing his Laptop.

After entering office, Vivi signed the attendance register and got settled in his cabin. He opened his inbox. Not to his surprise, he found seven mails. Four were from his boss and the rest were from the clients. He started to read the mails and to his dismay, all of the mails from his boss came attached with additional work. All this work belonged to Vivi's Boss, but the job was passed onto Vivi as always. He got pissed off; looking at the magnitude of the extra work he had to do. But he convinced himself saying that the completion of this additional work would enable him to get the leave he wanted. He started to gather data for the first overnight mail.

During the course of work, he remembered that he had left the leave request form at his Boss' table a couple of days ago. He wanted to check its status before he discussed it with him. He entered the Boss' cabin and started to browse through the files on the table. He found his file at the bottom of the pile, untouched. Sure that it had not been read, he replaced it at the top of the pile this time. After doing this, Vivi glanced at the condition of the table and the computer on it. It had not been cleaned since his Boss had left for a two day trip to his hometown. Vivi wondered why it had not been cleaned. He thought that the condition of the table and its dirt might annoy his Boss and this could also hamper the chances of getting his vacation sanctioned. Without a thought, Vivi started dusting the table and all the things around it. After cleaning the cabin to his satisfaction, when Vivi turned around, he saw his Boss entering the cabin.

"Good Morning, Sir!" said Vivi in a surprised voice.

"Good Morning. What are you spying in my cabin this early for?" asked the Boss in a casual yet authoritative voice.

"Nothing sir, I was just cleaning the table as it was way dirty," answered Vivi.

"Good, now that you have started doing the cleaning job too, I can cut down on one of the sub staff now!" ridiculed the Boss.

Vivi tried to divert the topic by asking the date of the company's regional conference.

"I am not sure about the date. I was informed that it could be postponed by a week's time!" answered the Boss.

Delighted with what he had heard Vivi thought that his vacation plan would not be a hindrance to his conference presentation after all. Keeping his happiness in check, Vivi asked, "So is it ok for you if I get the presentation ready by next week, sir?"

"No. You better finish it this week. You never know what goes on in these bastards' minds! They make decisions with their feet."

"Sir, but you have given me those report work for the inspection?"

"So what? You can do both simultaneously!" answered the Boss in a very casual tone.

Unable to offend his Boss by saying No, Vivi continued to remain silent.

Looking at the leave request at the top of the file, the Boss said, “Three days leave and that too from tomorrow? This is not possible!”

“Sir, I had already told you about this last week but you were too busy to make note of it!” replied Vivi.

“You don’t understand the seriousness of the situation and take leave without bothering about the company!” continued the Boss in a harsh tone.

“Sir, I have not taken a single day’s leave this quarter. I need this break very badly for my family!” replied Vivi.

“What about the presentation and all those inspection reports? Who will do all of those things?” asked the Boss.

“I will continue to work on it during the leave as well!” answered Vivi.

“I can’t trust you on that and that when you are on a vacation break. I must ask Ravi to take over from you then,” said the Boss.

Not wanting to give the advantage to Ravi, Vivi said, “Sir, I have already started working on the presentation. All the data is in my laptop and I am sure I can finish this work on time!”

Thinking for a while, the Boss looked at Vivi and said, “In that case I need your updates on the presentation everyday during your leave. You must finish the inspection report as well by the time you come back to office!”

Swallowing his happiness at the leave sanction, Vivi said, “Sure sir, I will definitely do it!”

“Remember, don’t switch off your phone and don’t give me excuses. I am taking a big risk here and I hope you understand that!”

"I understand, sir. I won't let you down!" said Vivi trying to get out of the room before his Boss came up with any more conditions.

Coming out of his Boss' cabin, Vivi called his wife and said, "Jenny, start packing the bags. We are leaving tomorrow!"

❁❁❁

The alarm rang at 7:00 AM. Forgetting it was a holiday; Vivi woke up and started thinking about office. Opening the front door, he took the day's newspaper and walked towards the kitchen looking for his tea. Failing to see both his wife and tea in the kitchen, Vivi got annoyed and started shouting for her.

"What happened?" asked Jenny, coming out of the bedroom.

"Where is my tea?" he shouted again.

"Can't you make it yourself at least today?"

"Why?" asked Vivi.

"Because today we are leaving for the vacation and I have better things to do!" said Jenny opening the closet for packing the remaining clothes for the vacation.

That was when it sank into Vivi's mind. "What was I thinking?" he asked himself and continued, "I definitely need this break!"

Vivi believed in doing things according to plan and this vacation was no exception. He had prepared a detailed sketch for the vacation starting from the ride from home till their return from the vacation. He had planned all the destinations that they would visit during their trip and booked the hotel for their stay. He bought extra batteries and memory cards for his camera and also some woolen clothes and a big umbrella. Vivi had planned the schedule for the vacation with specific times for each activity. Office work was also an integral part of the activity. Vivi made his tea in a hurry and glanced through the day's newspaper. He started packing his utilities in his backpack and his papers for the presentation. He had a quick shower and wore his long forgotten tees and jeans.

"I look smarter in this. I should wear it often!" Vivi said looking at Jenny.

"Then stop going to office on weekends," Jenny replied packing the final bag for the trip.

"You have a point!" admitted Vivi and continued, "You better hurry up and get Danny ready before it's late!"

"But it is just 8:30 and our train is only at 12:30!" Jenny said, annoyed.

"I know but I can't take chances with the traffic. Better go early and wait rather than be late and sorry!"

Jenny was irritated, but started to wake Danny up nevertheless. It was 9:30 AM when Vivi and family were all set for the trip. Vivi hired a cab and they began their journey to the railway station. The traffic was unexpectedly less and they reached the station at 10:10 AM. They couldn't find a decent place to sit and hence sat amidst a crowded pack. After sitting, Vivi opened his Laptop.

"I thought we are on a holiday. Please don't bore us with your office work again!" said Jenny in an agitated voice.

"This is important to me, Jenny, only because my agreeing to work on the trip, I was given this leave sanction!" explained Vivi.

"So what's the point of taking a break?" shouted Jenny.

"It's complicated. You won't understand," replied Vivi trying to silence Jenny.

Angered at Vivi's response, Jenny murmured, "I really don't know what happened to you after marriage. You've lost it all!"

"Oh really? I had to lose it all because I don't want to lose my job and the money it gives me to run my family!" shouted Vivi.

Stopping herself from saying anything more, Jenny rose from her seat and walked out to the book shop, taking Danny with her. She spent some time reading books and buying some coloring books for Danny. She went to the juice shop and finally spent some time at a fast food outlet in the station. Vivi was oblivious to everything that was happening around him and was glued to his laptop.

❋❋❋

In the train opposite to Vivi's family, a middle aged American couple was seated. Rachael, the American lady smiled at Jenny and was well reciprocated by Jenny. They casually started the conversation about raising the child and the precautions they need to take care of. Then the conversation started about their journey and their plans for the trip.

"So are you guys visiting India for the first time?" Jenny asked.

"No, this is the second time. We covered south India in our previous trip. This time it is the North East!" said Rachael.

"That's great, we haven't seen south India yet!" said Jenny.

"Then you must plan to, soon. You will have a lot of fun, believe me. If you want, I can show you the pictures of our previous visit!" suggested Rachael.

"I would love to see them!" smiled Jenny. The women started looking at the pictures and their discussion continued.

Getting bored of sitting idly, Andy, the American man, looked at Vivi and broke the ice. "Have you made arrangements for your stay?"

"Yes, I did it 20 days ago!" answered Vivi showcasing his preparedness for the trip.

"That's great. Our trip is totally unplanned. We decided on this trip only yesterday and today we are here with you!" said Andy with a little smile.

"What about the stay?" asked Vivi with concern.

"We shall see that once we reach there. We have not zeroed on our destinations yet. We thought of going with the flow!" answered Andy with ease.

"That sounds interesting!" said Vivi with a sarcastic smile.

"So what are your plans for the trip?" asked Andy trying to build up on the conversation.

"Since you asked, let me show my excel file!" answered Vivi opening up his laptop. Vivi showed Andy the trip plan which included timings for breakfast, lunch and dinner.

"Unbelievable. I think you must have almost lived the trip while making this sheet!" answered Andy in amazement looking at the excel file.

"I told you, I believe in making plans and living them!" boasted Vivi.

"But tell me one thing, how come you plan the timing of your food as well?" asked Andy in amazement.

"What's wrong with that? This helps me to keep the focus on the overall plan!"

"I hardly end up eating on time while travelling. I remember our last trip where I was engrossed in a book at the beach, sipping lemon juice all day long!" said Andy.

Not amazed at Andy's reply Vivi said, "I don't read books when I travel. I think it is waste of time, at least during the vacation!"

Unaware of the sarcasm that Vivi hinted at, Andy asked, looking at the file, "What's that presentation written in the file?"

"Well, that's some personal work which I have planned for myself. So how often do you visit places?" Vivi asked, trying to distract from the topic.

"We go for an overseas trip twice a year. We make sure that we take a little break every month to visit places within the country!"

"That's good. You should be making a lot of money to do that!" said Vivi, trying to ask Andy about his career indirectly.

"Well, I can only wish for it. Most of my money ends in paying for the trips and whatever Rachael makes, we spend for the family!" said Andy.

"What about the savings then?"

"I am not much of a savings person and neither is Rachael. But I do have the maximum possible insurance!" answered Andy.

Finding the conversation interesting, Vivi said, "What about the savings for your children?"

"Well, we have not thought about it so far. Maybe in the future we might consider it!"

"If you ask me, you better consider it early before it's too late!" said Vivi, trying to be a well-wisher.

"Yeah, sure!" answered Andy. "I assume you must be a good investor. Will need your advice sometime!" continued Andy in a friendly tone.

"Anytime, but believe me, the best advice given to me to double my money was to fold it into half and put it back into my pocket!"

"Well said. I can only start working on the folding part as of now!" said Andy laughing at the joke

Vivi asked, "So tell me what you do?"

"Well, I am a plumber. Off late, I've started working on carpentry as well!"

Startled by Andy's reply, Vivi asked in amazement, "So with the money you make, can you afford these trips?"

"Yeah! I must admit that we restrict ourselves to economy flights and budget hotels!"

"Do you mean to say that you don't have a regular job?" Vivi asked.

"Yeah you can say that to some extent!" answered Andy.

"Why do you spend your money on all these trips? Believe it or not, this is my first outing in two years!" answered Vivi trying to help Andy.

"That's a tough call to make. These trips or rather breaks, help me and Rachael gain some sense of personal conscience. The other day, we were discussing that these trips help us see ourselves more than anything else!" said Andy.

Surprised by this unexpected response, Vivi said, "That's an interesting perspective to look at but I look at it only on the fun angle!"

Smiling, Andy said, "I believe fun is a general word. When I said conscience, I meant understanding me and the things that makes me happy!"

Understanding that the subject was getting deeper than he had anticipated, Vivi pulled out his new SLR camera to take a picture of the landscapes from the window.

"That's a nice camera you've got!" said Andy looking at Vivi.

"Thank you. This cost me a fortune but it's worth every penny!" replied Vivi unpacking the batteries safely. "By the way, what camera do you use?" asked Vivi.

"I am not a camera person. Rachael takes pictures for her album but I try to live the moment and do not believe in capturing it in a chip!"

"I must admit, you are a very interesting person!" said Vivi.

Sensing that he had wasted a lot of time on a futile discussion, Vivi excused himself from Andy saying that he had some letters to type and started working on his presentation work without a delay. Vivi continued to work for a couple of hours when his new found friends settled down on their berth for a quick nap. He looked at his wife who was busy feeding Danny with snacks and told her in a low voice, "Look at these people, they look rich but they are actually losers!"

"How do you say that?" asked Jenny maintaining the same tone.

"They don't have any savings, they don't have any children and they still roam around like gypsies!"

"But they are still happy, don't you think so?"

"But this is just a present situation. What will happen to them when they grow old?" asked back Vivi.

"I don't know. But I believe that with the attitude they have, they will continue to remain happy forever, unlike us!" said Jenny.

"What? What do you mean by unlike us?"

"We think too much about our retirement than about our present. We hardly make special memories and everyday is just the same. Speaking about savings, most of our earnings are gone in EMI's!" said Jenny much to Vivi's dissatisfaction.

"Do you think I am doing that for myself? I am doing it for you. I try to ensure that as long as I am in this job, I make the most out of it. If I lose this job then can you imagine what will happen to us?" asked Vivi.

"What bad can happen? You will find a new job! If not, I will help you and we will do some business. Why fear? It is affecting your personality, Vivi!" answered Jenny.

"Don't jump to conclusions. I am not afraid, but concerned. Anyway you won't understand it!" said Vivi in haste and got his focus back on to the laptop.

The journey continued till the train reached the hill station at 3:00 in the morning. Vivi and his family took their bags and accessories and got off. Vivi realized that Andy and Jennifer were carrying a single backpack each and thought how unprepared were they for a trip like this. Andy and Jenny bid goodbye and left.

Vivi reached the hotel and told the receptionist about the booking he had made at one of their city offices and showed his driving license as the ID proof. The receptionist requested for the payment receipt as the payment was not shown online. Vivi looked in his bag only to realize that he had forgotten to carry the receipt. He was worried and kept searching the bag as if he would find it by some miracle. Meanwhile, Jenny asked the receptionist to allow them, since they had forgotten to carry the receipt with them. Considering the kid with the couple and a sweet request from Jenny, the receptionist made an exception and welcomed them to their hotel. The family entered their room and jumped into bed without a delay.

The next morning, Vivi made sure everyone got ready by 9:00 AM so that they didn't miss the free breakfast. After breakfast, they geared up for their first destination, Park Lake. Vivi booked a cab for the day and their ride started with a beautiful hillside view. Just as the journey began, Vivi opened his laptop trying not to waste time. Once in a while, he peeped out of the windows to take pictures. As the cab began to descend from the mountains slope, Vivi's phone rang. It was his Boss' call. Perturbed by the sudden call, Vivi asked the driver to halt the cab. He got out of the car to answer the call.

"Good Morning, Sir! I was about to call you in sometime," said Vivi.

"Mmmm, so how's the progress?" asked the boss.

"I am halfway through it, sir. I shall mail you the developments by the evening!" answered Vivi.

"That's too late. Send them now."

"Sure Sir. I will do it now," answered Vivi with no resistance.

The Boss abruptly disconnected the call without waiting for Vivi to complete his statement. After getting into the car, Vivi ordered the driver to take him to a nearby internet centre as his data card was not working.

"Are you aware we are on a vacation?" Jenny asked angrily.

"Please don't disturb me now. It is important!" answered Vivi copying the presentation file into his pen drive. The driver had to make a big return trip around the hill station trying to find an internet centre. He found a small facility beside the main market. Vivi promised Jenny that he would take just five minutes to finish the work and rushed to the internet centre. Much to his annoyance the internet speed was way too slow and it had consumed almost an hour of Vivi's time. When Vivi came out of the centre, he was two hours behind his scheduled plan. He got into the cab and spent most of the time trying to pacify Jenny as they headed towards the lake. When they reached the Lake, it was lunch time already. Vivi thought of taking Jenny to a good restaurant and asked the driver for his suggestions. The driver hinted at the lake restaurant which was situated at the lake shore. Vivi decided to go to the restaurant to finish lunch first. Just as they were about to pass through the lake, they saw Andy and Jennifer coming out of a small hut resort besides the lake.

"What a surprise!" exclaimed Andy looking at Vivi.

"For us, too!" answered Vivi. "So are you staying here?"

"You bet! This is a house, actually! We saw this place when we were on our way towards the city. It looked beautiful and without waiting, we got in and asked for place to stay. As the owners were out of town, the watchman had agreed for a small tip!" smiled Andy.

Looking at the amazing location of the hut, Vivi said, "Lucky you!"

Both the families proceeded for lunch together. When Vivi was analyzing the menu, Jenny ordered for her favorite prawn curry and chicken noodles for Danny. Andy called on the waiter and said, "Get me two plates of your restaurant's specialty!"

Surprised at Andy's order, Vivi asked him, "Do you know the restaurant's specialty already?"

Andy smilingly said, "No, but this is my regular order at any new restaurant. By doing this, I ensure that the restaurant will try to live up to its specialty or even otherwise I shall taste a new adventure!"

"Good one, I must try it next time!" answered Vivi later realizing that he should also enquire the price of the specialty before the order. After a hearty lunch, Vivi and his family went boating in the lake. Andy and Rachael left for the waterfalls nearby. Vivi chose a motorboat for the ride as he believed that he could save some time and energy with it over a pedaling boat. After spending a couple of hours at the lake, Vivi took the family to the children's park nearby, to entertain Danny and engage Jenny. This would also give him some time for his office work. By the time they returned from the park, it got dark.

"So should we head back to the hotel?" asked Jenny.

Closing his laptop immediately, Vivi said, "Not that soon dear, we still have the waterfalls in our schedule!"

"But it's already late!"

"That's what I call adventure!" answered Vivi with a new found smile after finishing a good deal of office work.

"As you wish," acknowledged Jenny trying not to disappoint Vivi with his plans. By the time Vivi reached the waterfalls, the sun had already set. The full moon light provided a special spark to the falling water. With no one at the venue, the place looked like a dream. They approached the falls, holding each other's hands. Just as they were about to reach the falls, the flowing water pulled out the watch from Vivi's arms into the water. Unable to lose the costly watch which his wife had given him, Vivi made his way towards the stream trying to find it. Vivi found his watch supported on a tree's branch, against the stream of running water.

Just when he was about to grab it, he heard Jenny shouting at the top of her voice, "Danny! Vivi catch Danny! Vivi catch Danny!"

Shocked at the shouts, Vivi turned around to realize that Danny had jumped into the water and was being carried away with it. With all his might, Vivi rushed against the opposing stream but lost balance when he put his foot into a deep gap between the stones. Disoriented, Vivi couldn't move ahead and was also pushed into the water body. He kept shouting, "Danny, I am coming, I am coming!" He could not resist being pushed away by the mighty water current.

Every time Vivi tried to come out of the water, he kept hitting his head against the rocks. Vivi's worst fears grew. His life started to flash in front of his eyes. He tried to shout but he felt his voice being muted by the roaring waters. When Vivi tried to regain balance, he realized that he was about to fall from a steep mountain. Finding his power to resist diminishing against the raging waters, Vivi's mind went blank.

Closing his eyes he shouted, "God give me a chance. GODDDD!"

Vivi fell from a 200 feet high mountain into deep water, surrounded by dense trees.

❁❁❁

When Vivi regained his consciousness, he felt pain across his back. He was in a state of delusion; his eyes were open but not his vision. He felt something stopping him from moving and pulling him down. He saw his legs bleeding profusely and was unable to bear the pain which radiated all over his body. Suddenly, he realized that he was alive and in that instant, he found solace amidst pain. He remembered his son and his heart started to pound faster. He did not know what to do as his movement was totally curtailed by unbearable pain. He looked around, and it was very dark. He tried to focus and this time, he realized he was inside a small dark room without any windows. The room had a single iron door which was rusted and black. When he tried to make a move towards the door he found that his legs were tied together by an iron chain. That instant, Vivi started to fear. He was unable to find a reason for the situation. He realized that somebody must have saved him but his present state inside the room confused him. He began to fear that he was already dead and was in hell. He started to think about all that could have happened to his son and began to cry at the thought of the negative possibilities. His mind started to waver and his fear started to increase with every passing second.

With nothing to stop the pain and nobody around, he began shouting for help. Initially he started to shout for help but over time he began shouting for his wife, child and finally God. But the place remained quiet. He was furious and started to yell more and more, but there was no response. Unable to bear the pain, Vivi lay down on his back trying to relax his injured body. He started speaking to himself. He started to pacify him saying that this was a dream and he would soon wake up. He also started to wonder when his dream must have started. Is this whole vacation a dream or is he dreaming during the vacation? With all these confusing thoughts striking him repeatedly, Vivi lost his mind and became weak and defenseless. He slowly drifted off to sleep in the tiny cell, unaware of the surroundings.

Vivi suddenly woke up when he heard a loud thud outside. He immediately felt that he was not dreaming anymore and something serious was happening around him. The heavy iron doors opened and two dark men entered the cell, carrying an injured person. They threw him on the floor and stared at Vivi.

One person who was bare-chested shouted at Vivi, "Listen to us or else you will die!"

Shocked at the sight of the men and the sound of their angry voices, Vivi was unable to react and kept mum. He shook his head as if he understood everything they said. After the warning, the two men tied the legs of the wounded person with a chain and left the cell. Vivi's situation worsened. He thought he was lucky to be alive, but now he was inside a dreaded cell with dangerous men around waiting to kill him. To add to this, he sat next to a possibly dying or perhaps even dead man. Vivi closed his eyes and started praying to the almighty. His prayers got longer as he repeated them. He prayed for his son's life first, then his life, then for his family and finally prayed for his early freedom to make it on time for his office presentation.

After an hour of praying, he opened his eyes and to his horror he saw the wounded stranger sitting opposite him, resting against the wall.

The stranger smiled at Vivi and said, "You are one hell of a coward!"

Not able to digest the comment passed, Vivi said, "Everyone gets only one life and I need my life for my family. If you consider this cowardly, that's not my problem!"

Smiling again, the stranger said, "To live, you need more courage than this. By the way I also heard your prayers for the job promotion. You better prioritize your wishes before the God gets confused!"

Not trying to answer the stranger's sarcastic remark, Vivi said, "Please leave me and my prayers alone. Do you know where we are and why are we chained?"

Stopping his smile, the stranger said, "Why do you think these tribes have locked us? They want their leader to be freed from prison and in return we get to live our remaining lives!"

"What?" Vivi was stunned, and asked, "But why us?"

"Maybe they know that we each have a loving family who can free their leader," answered the stranger.

Vivi stopped speaking and remained calm for some time. The sequence of events, he thought, was possible only in a movie. He felt something had gone terribly wrong. Otherwise, how can this happen to a simple person like him? He began to cry when he started the think of the fate of his little child.

"Stop crying!" shouted the stranger. "You better think of a solution or face the death like a man, but don't cry like a baby asking for milk"

"What are you, human or something else? Don't you have emotions? I have lost my only son to the bloody waters and I am sitting here getting ready to die. All I can see is my loving wife crying for the rest of her life!" Vivi said in an angry voice.

"I still say the same thing. Worrying can't help you. If you are determined to be sad then no one can help you. It can only make you weaker and nothing else!" answered the stranger.

"So what choice do I have sitting in this stinking filthy room?"

"The only thing you can do and you must do is to get rid of the day alive and nothing else," said the stranger in a serious tone.

Vivi calmed down for a moment trying not to get hyper again. He gathered his wits and asked, "And what about tomorrow?"

"That will be seen tomorrow. You are alive now so you better think of passing this day without wasting much energy. Today's strength and patience can help you face tomorrow," said the stranger.

"And how do you know that?" asked Vivi.

"Well, I live my life that way. I call it 'Not Today'!"

"Seriously? When was the last time you used your motto?" asked Vivi, intentionally trying to divert his mind away from the seriousness of the situation.

"Well, if you are interested, I can tell you about an interesting situation when I used this motto," said the stranger.

Vivi nodded.

The stranger said, "To begin with, my name is Amar and I am a sailor. I used to work for a Greek shipping company which was renowned for buying scrap ships at cheap prices and then reconditioning them so they can be used for commercial purposes.

I was working on one such ship which was making its voyage from South Africa to North America. We were carrying crude oil cargo from Africa to America. Cargo discharge was done in three different American ports. American port authorities are very strict when it comes to the oil leakage from the ship as it pollutes their shore. In one discharging, we found that oil traces were coming out of the Engine room bilge outlet and this got the attention of the officers at the shore. They immediately entered the ship and warned of a possible arrest of the crew if the leakage was not rectified. The crew at the Engine room got urgent orders to trace the leakage and arrest it immediately. I was forced to wake up from the middle of my sleep to trace the leakage. I put on the boiler suit and the ear muffs and entered the engine room, way too tired. I was trying to locate the leakage inside the bilge space along with six other crewmen. Even after two hours of tracking, we were unable to trace the source of oil spill. The port authorities as well as the Captain entered the Engine room to look for any progress. That is when I shouted "I found it, I found it". I took a broken oil seal ring lying below the bilge pump which pumps out the oil into the sea and started running towards the Captain. "This is the culprit Captain; the leakage will be stopped once we replace it!" The Captain was impressed with my detection and he convinced the port authorities who were standing beside him that the oil spill will be stopped and that they need not take any action against the ship and its crew. The port authorities granted the sanction to continue the discharge. After replacing the oil ring, the oil traces were still found. But I convinced the authorities that those were the residual oil remains and it would stop in sometime. After that our ship continued its journey to the next port."

"That's interesting. You mean to say that you actually fooled the Captain as well as the authorities?" asked Vivi.

"I tried to locate the leakage but time was ticking. In shipping, time is money and any delay can cost us dearly!"

"So did you use the same technique in the next port also?" asked Vivi.

"You bet! But this time, I located an imaginary crack in the bilge space," said Amar looking at Vivi's keen face.

"What about the Captain? Didn't he realize you were tricking them?" asked Vivi.

"He realized it, but he had no other option but to act along with me to save time and money!"

"So did you finally end up tracing the leakage or not?" Vivi asked.

"At the third discharge port, the Captain acted better than I did and in the final discharge port we finally found the leakage!" said Amar.

"Nice!" said Vivi.

"Now, you see, all I had to do was pass the day or the situation and I was sure the next day will be better!" explained Amar finishing his tale.

"Mmm, first let me get out of this place alive!" said Vivi who was more relaxed after the discussion. He started to find solace in speaking with Amar and he somehow felt that he was getting into a positive mindset.

They continued their discussion for some more time and after that, both decided to rest. They were not sure if it was night or day, however their loaded eyelids made them decide it had to be night. While they were asleep, the iron door creaked again and this time, a tiny person entered the cell with two plates and a water bottle in hand. He threw them on the floor, waking up Vivi and Amar.

"Take your food!" shouted the person and left the cell.

Each plate carried two dry breads which were now scattered on the floor. The bread was dark and it was way beyond edible but Vivi knew that they had no choice.

Amar took a slice from the floor and bit into it. He joked, “Looks like this bread has been prepared specially for us. Lot of effort has gone into its colour and flavor!”

Vivi smiled and took his first bite. While they were eating, they heard a loud gun shot.

Vivi was shocked. “Are they killing people?”

“Sounds like that,” Amar answered, continuing to bite his dry food.

“Will they kill us?” asked Vivi losing all the positivity he had gathered in the past few hours.

“Don’t fear about things over which you don’t have control!”

“But do I have any other choice?” Vivi asked again.

“Like I said before, just pass this day by hook or by crook!”

Vivi lay down, closing his eyes trying not to think anymore but the thought of his kid and his wife kept worrying him over and over again.

After staying quiet for a while, Vivi asked Amar, “What do you do to control your fear and worry?”

“I keep thinking of the happy times of my life or else I create some happy dreams!”

“You seem to have answer for everything,” Vivi said.

“It’s my solitude that forced my mind to create imaginative ways to escape it!”

“Do you have a family?”

Amar paused for a moment and looking away from Vivi, he said, “I lost them all!”

Vivi was taken aback by the reply. The perception of Amar in Vivi’s mind changed immediately. He wondered how a person with so much loss gave him so much confidence. Vivi decided not to trouble Amar anymore with his questions and kept mum.

The calmness in the cell and the tiredness of the souls superseded Vivi's physical pain. He slept through the entire night, forgetting everything around them.

Morning arrived and Vivi was still fast asleep whereas Amar was wide awake. The door opened again but this time, rashly. Two men entered the cell. They dragged Vivi and Amar out of the cell. Vivi dreaded it. He cried for help but Amar remained calm all the while. The black men continued to drag the helpless people for some more distance till they reached an open ground in the middle of the forest. Once they reached the centre of the open ground, the two of them were thrown onto the ground, with their legs still tied together by the chain.

With a lot of difficulty Vivi tried to stand up and saw that he was surrounded by six dark men, each holding a rifle in their hands. He saw another captive lying with his legs chained. He was an old man with long white hair covering his face. Trying not to focus on anything, Vivi started to beg for his life. Amar remained silent from the time he was pulled out of the cell. The old man was making funny gestures and was looking around like he was a mentally challenged person.

Once the six men with their rifles had assembled in the open field with their captives, their captain emerged from the woods wearing a green uniform. He closed in on the captives and looked directly into their eyes. He said, "We have nothing against you but we need our leader. So you have to act according to our orders or else, you know what will happen. First, we will be recording your video in which you will beg for your life. You must say great things about our leader and mention that the police have made a mistake in arresting him. You must keep begging for your life, all the time, and if any of you try to act smart, I won't hesitate to pull the trigger. I have already filled up one of our empty graves with a young boy's body yesterday."

Vivi started to worry about the possibilities of the young boy being his son. But he could not gain courage to ask. He felt his legs shiver like never before and felt a chill throughout his body.

The Captain continued, "So can all of you start begging or do you want us to make you beg?"

"Was your leader a social worker?" Amar asked in a bold voice.

"What? What did you say?" asked the Captain, surprised by the audacity of the captive.

"I am telling you that your leader, who destroyed a village by killing its people and raping its daughters, is basically a fucking animal and not a social worker!" said Amar in a clear bold voice again.

"How dare you say that?" shouted the Captain.

"When you misfits in society can speak so boldly, why can't a civilized common man do the same?" replied Amar, clearly not willing to stop.

The Captain got wild at Amar's attitude and kicked his face with all his might.

Amar was thrown back with blood dripping from his mouth.

Coming closer to Amar, the Captain asked again, "Do you have a different opinion now?"

Amar without any hesitation replied, "My opinions are not based on fear and you animals can't make any difference to them!"

The Captain could not believe what he was hearing. With all his might, he kicked Amar to vent out all his anger.

Continuing to kick, he shouted at Amar, "Don't you need life to save your family, bastard? Don't you have a family to go back to, bastard? Won't your kid wait for your return, bastard?"

Amar shouted back, "Good to know that you understand family too. Maybe you have one as well. Please don't tell your kid what you do for a living! Please ask your wife to make food with her earnings and please do taste it once!"

The Captain stopped kicking. He asked one of his people to get the camera and to start recording the video. He placed his rifle on Amar's head and asked, "Any final wish?"

Amar, in a clear and unperturbed voice, said, "You idiots! Stop fucking around and start living a real life!"

The trigger was pulled and Amar dropped dead.

"The Lion died today and the sheep are dying every day!" shouted the chained old man, clapping his hands and running in circles around the dead Amar. Vivi's mind went blank. It was the first time he saw death in front of his eyes and that too of a person he had begun to look upon as a friend and guide. Vivi could neither cry nor think. He was yet to understand what had happened before him. He stood there with the chains, looking blankly at the bleeding corpse, which still had its eyes open.

"So who's next?" asked the Captain looking at Vivi.

"No sir, I will do as you say sir!" Vivi replied, shivering.

"Then follow the instructions and save your life," he said and left the spot.

Vivi did exactly as per the instructions given to him. He cried, begged and praised the so-called leader in front of the camera. The old man was unable to understand anything that was said to him. He kept smiling and looking at everybody with a smile which irritated the men. They thought he was of no use to them; but they decided to retain him just in case somebody identified him in the video and tried for his release. After recording the video, both captives were dragged back and thrown into the same cell. Vivi continued to lie on the floor, unable to comprehend the situation as he continued shivering. The old man, on the other hand, made loud bizarre noises and hit the chain forcefully on the ground. It disturbed Vivi.

The death of his friend indicated that his death couldn't be far. He began to sweat. He thought about the young dead boy that the killer had mentioned. He started to worry for his son.

He thought of his wife and what would happen to her if he died. He wondered if the recorded video would reach the police and what would happen if the police refused to release the leader. His mind was wavering. He woke up and walked up and down the tiny cell. The iron chains restricted his movement but it didn't restrict his coagulated mind. The old man, irrespective of the seriousness of the situation, kept banging the chains and shouting. Vivi lay down again and began praying for his son and wife. He cried, slept and woke up again, and walked up and down. He was restless. He started crying and said, "Please help me! I will give you everything I have. Please let me see my wife and my child again. I will come back to you!"

His pleas fell on deaf ears. The old man's noises irritated him but he knew there was nothing he could do to stop it. Vivi looked around and saw that the place had nothing but a dim light on top. Vivi shouted again, "I am sorry, Jenny! I have been a hopeless husband and careless dad. You deserve a better person than me. I am going to die, Jenny. I am sorry, Jenny. I am sorry, Jenny. Please forgive me, Jenny. Please forgive me."

Saying these words Vivi banged his wrist on the wall with full force. His arms felt a sharp pain after the first hit but that did not deter him from hitting the wall again and again until his knuckles began to bleed. He tried kicking the wall, but slipped and fell face first on the floor. With his lips bleeding, he got up and started walking faster and shouting his apology repeatedly like a maniac. Every time Vivi shouted, the old man banged his chain harder on the floor, making the noises louder. Finally, Vivi stopped and moved to the corner of the cell and sat down, resting his back on the wall. Tears poured out of his tired eyes. Seeing the old man making uninterrupted noise, he shouted at him. "Stop making those fucking noises, you moron! I have been dying all my life and I am again going to die tomorrow! Let me die in peace!"

The old man paused for a second, he looked at Vivi and he smiled. He started banging the chain again and this time much louder.

"I should have been a retard like you, my life would have been better!" Vivi cursed himself.

The old man looked at Vivi and laughed sarcastically.

"Laugh out loudly, you maniac. Remember, you are not the first to laugh at me. My friends laughed at me when I stammered, my parents laughed at me when I wanted to be an actor, my crush laughed at me when I proposed to her, my teacher laughed at me when I asked her questions and my relatives laughed at me when I wanted to start my own company. All these things made me a maniac too! Otherwise, why would I work like a donkey at a dirty job? Now even my wife and child will laugh at me for being who I am and not what I wanted to become!"

The old man continued to look at Vivi with a funny face. Vivi looked at the old man with a tired expression. He felt weak and defenseless. He wanted to meet his wife and child before dying. Unable to concentrate on anything anymore, he closed his eyes. The fatigue made him sleep with blood still dripping from his lips and arms. Unperturbed by the old man's noise, Vivi slept deeply, for long. He was unaware of the dry lunch that was thrown into the cell, at him. He was unaware of the new videos that were recorded of him when he was sleeping, bleeding. It was almost dark when Vivi woke up. He saw the dry bread and bent plates on the floor. He realized that he must have slept for a long time. He glanced at the old man who sat silently with his eyes closed. The old man was smiling as if he was in a happy and detached state. Vivi remained silent. He accepted his defeat and was mentally getting ready to die.

The door of the cell opened and the Captain entered the room. He looked at the condition of his captives. He kicked the old man to get his attention. The old man stared at him. It did not bother the Captain as he never took the old man seriously. Looking at Vivi, the Captain said, "Your videos have been handed over to the police and we haven't received any communication from them so far. It seems that they are not taking us serious enough. This is not good news for you. We have given the police time till 9:00 AM tomorrow and if our leader is not released by then, we will be left with no other choice but to kill you. If you think we need you for the blackmail, let me tell you, it is not difficult for us to find new scape goats!"

Vivi cried, "Sir, please let me see my family once. Please sir!"

"Shut up!" shouted the Captain. "Don't think that we will be moved by your tears. We live for a mission and your life is just a means to achieve it!"

The Captain took a pen and a few sheets of paper from his pocket and threw it at Vivi. "This might be your last night of your life and if you have anything to tell the family, put it on paper. This will be placed on your dead body when it is delivered to your family!" saying these words, he left the cell.

Vivi kept looking at the papers on the floor. He had lost all hope when he heard that it could be the last night of his life. He picked up the sheets of paper from the floor and settled down on one corner of the room. His hands began to tremble when he picked up the pen to write. He knew that this was his last chance to say all that that he ever wanted to tell jenny. Gathering his composure, Vivi started to write.

Dear Love,

I am writing this, sitting inside a tiny cell awaiting my death and this might be the last time that I would ever write to you. I pray to God that Danny is with you, when you are reading this. If anything had happened to him, then I deserve this death more than anything else.

I feel responsible for everything that is happening. I am sorry, Jenny, I am really sorry. Please forgive me. You are everything to me and when I realize I am going to die leaving you alone, I just can't bear it. You should not lose track of your life after my death. My death is because of me and there is absolutely no fault of yours.

Sitting in this cell, I realized how blessed I was to have an amazing wife like you. Rather than living the life with you, I have been running an unconscious race missing out on all the charms of life. I wonder how a girl like you could bear a loser like me all this while. I don't understand why I kept shouting at you for all the little things. I don't understand why I did not encourage you when you wanted to study more. I don't understand why I did not help you in your daily work.

You never got angry when I refused to take you out and even if you did get angry you didn't let it disturb me. I missed out on the birthdays and anniversaries and you still surprised me on all occasions. Why do you love me so much, Jenny? I don't deserve this. I want to hug you and tell that it's all a dream but I cannot.

I keep thinking of the happy hug Danny gives me when I come home. I did not realize how much it meant to him then, but now I do. I remember his joyous smile when I took him for a little bike ride. I should have done that more often rather than wasting time on that futile newspaper. I wasted my precious time in office trying to please those rotten bosses. I should have taken you to the park everyday in the evenings rather than doing extra work for my boss. I had taken you for granted whereas it is you who complete my life. How stupid of me to mess up my priorities in life!

I was a coward all my life. My fear reduced my life to misery. I was robbed of my genuine happiness. I wanted to be in the comfort zone all the time and never took chances with anything. When I wonder what is the worst thing that could have happened to me, had I gotten out of my comfort zone, I realize that it might have been that, I would not have gotten a good place to stay, good food to eat, good bed to sleep, good health to live, good company to speak, good music to listen, good neighbor to interact and good mind to think. Sitting in this cell I realize that I am in the exact same zone which I had dreaded all this while. But even then, I am not bothered about it. All that matters to me is an extra day with you and Danny!

I am lost, Jenny. I am totally lost. More than the conditions here, it is the mistakes of my life that haunt me repeatedly. Please forgive me for everything. I had so many plans for our family but when I realize all of it is going to disappear, it makes me believe that there is nothing like God. Please take care. I wish I could go back and make a fresh start, but I cannot. I have killed half of my life already by my fear and the rest will be killed tomorrow. I am sorry, Jenny; I wish I could express my love for you and Danny. I wish I could hug you both and say goodbye. But I can't. Please live a happy life Jenny and make my soul rest in peace.

Thank you for your unconditional love. I will miss you both.

Vivian John

❁❁❁

It was 10: 00 PM when the Captain entered the room with some special food for the captives.

Looking at Vivi, he said, "Enjoy your final dinner!"

Vivi pleaded with a broken voice, "I am ready to die, but please let me meet my wife and my kid once. I beg you."

"Stop asking for this. You know I won't do it. If you have any other last wish then let me know!" answered the Captain trying to show some mercy.

"Outside, outside!" shouted the old man, jumping up and down.

"What?" The Captain asked seeing the old man's excitement.

"My last wish, take me outside, take me outside!" jumped the old man again conveying his last wish.

The Captain thought for a second. He looked at Vivi and asked, "Do you want to come out too?"

Vivi said nothing and kept looking at the Leader with pitiful eyes. The Captain ordered his men to get the two captives outside and tie them to the trees near their camp. Both Vivi and the Old man were brought out of their cell to the camping area where a group of men including the Captain enjoyed a camp fire with alcohol. The men were already drunk and when they saw their captives being brought to their camping area, they shouted and ridiculed them. Vivi was angry with the old man for his stupid wish which had brought him near the deadly killers. After bringing Vivi and the Old man near the camping spot, the chains were removed from one of their legs to tie them to a tree nearby. While tying the chain to the trees, the old man shouted, "I want that chain. I want that chain!" pointing at Vivian's chain.

The men stopped tying and looked at Vivian's chain. It looked pretty new compared to the old man's chain. They looked at their Captain.

Laughing loud the Captain said, "Who found this guy in the jungle? He is the worst catch ever. Go on; make the fool happy again!"

As per the wish the chains were interchanged and then they were tied to the captives and the trees. Vivi and the old man sat far from the camp fire and couldn't feel the warmth of the fire. The chill weather with a damaged body was the worst nightmare for Vivi. He kept cursing the old Man for his wish and kept shivering all the while. The Captain and his men were partying hard and they were making plans for the next day. The Captain was upset with what Amar had said to him earlier that day before dying and that thought made him drink more. He looked at Vivi and threw an empty bottle at him, hitting his body. He cursed Vivi for Amar's act and kept on throwing bottles at him. Vivi tried escaping the bottles with his hands as they were free of any chains. He however got badly hit on his already injured arm which instantly got swollen. Vivi could not bear the pain, nor could he shout to kindle the captain's anger. He kept controlling his pain however his eyes continued to weep.

It was almost midnight when all the men including the Captain started to lose their consciousness to alcohol and started to doze. While everyone slept near the camp fire, the Captain closed in near Vivi and lay flat with a woolen blanket over him. Vivi succumbed to sleep as well. It was more of an unconsciousness state than real sleep. It was 3:00 AM. All the men and Vivi were fast asleep when Vivi felt a blow on his shoulders. He refused to react and continued to sleep despite the pain. He felt another strong blow and this time Vivi could not bear the pain and he turned around. It was the old man who was kicking Vivi sitting at a distance. He indicated to Vivi to keep his mouth shut. He threw a crushed piece of paper near Vivi, but he was unable to comprehend what the old man was trying to do. He bent and picked the paper.

He opened the paper and it read, "The seventh link of your chain from one end is broken. Once free, walk to the back of the cell where we were locked and start moving north. Walk slowly holding you chain for 20 minutes and then run!"

Vivi could not believe what he was reading. His tiredness and pain vanished. His heart began to beat faster. He read it again and looked at the old man. The old man signaled to remain silent and signaled him to work on his chain. Vivi slowly counted the seventh link of the chain from his hand and to his disappointment, he couldn't find anything broken. He then began to start counting from the tree and to his amazement he saw the seventh link from the tree was indeed broken. He slowly skid his chain through the broken gap and the whole chain came out like magic. He stood a free man. He came close to the old man to thank him but the old man signaled him to escape. Vivi held the chain up in his hands to prevent it from making any noise and started to move towards the back of the cell. With every step, he could hear his heart pounding. He kept moving till he reached the cell. He looked back at the old man from the cell. The old man showed a thumbs-up and signaled to him to keep moving. Vivi slowly reached the cell and started moving north. He had lost sense of time and was not sure how much time must have passed when he started his escape.

Irrespective of the time, he continued to move slowly. The jungle made it harder for him to navigate, however the moonlight gave him solace with its occasional light between the dense trees.

Vivi continued to walk slowly, holding his chain for more than 45 minutes. When he was passing through a tiny stream in the woods, he heard a sharp noise behind him. Vivi's heart skipped a beat, he forgot everything, and started to run. He did not bother to turn back. He continued to run as he knew this was his last chance to live. He ran across the bushes hurting his feet and legs, but hardly felt anything. He ran like a mad horse trying to cross all boundaries. He jumped the streams and maneuvered through the dense woods. He ran the whole night and his energy never ceased. His mind had no other thoughts but to run and run more.

It was almost 6:00 AM when Vivi realized that the woods were getting thinner. He was approaching the city. After a few more minutes of running, Vivi realized that he was standing on the exact road which had lead him to the dreaded waterfalls. Knowing which way to move, he continued to run despite being in the safe zone. He started seeing people and buses moving around and yet continued to run towards his hotel. Vivi started to feel that his mind was going blank and his legs were becoming numb. He looked around and saw the Police Station in the corner of the road. He stopped running and bent down, taking a deep breath. He decided to go to the police first and started limping towards the police station with a broken wrist and a bleeding face. Vivi fell on his knees on reaching the Police Station. He cried, "Inspector, help me. I am injured. I may collapse anytime. Please tell my wife that I am alive. Help me sir!"

"Vivi!" shouted the voice from the station. Jenny came running towards the door. Looking at Vivi, she hugged him and cried, "I knew you will come back. I knew you will come back!" she cried inconsolably.

Vivi's eyes brightened. He was seeing a dream in front of his eyes. He felt blessed to hold her in her arms and to kiss her forehead. Before Vivi could speak anything he saw Danny sleeping on the Inspector's table. Vivi felt ripples passing throughout his body and he realized what real happiness is.

"Andy saved Danny that day! Before he could reach you, you were gone!" said Jenny wiping her tears.

Vivi kept telling himself, "You got your second chance. You got your second chance!"

He pulled Danny and Jenny together and gave them a big hug and said, "I missed you. I love you more than anything else."

After the trauma, Vivi realized there was nothing more important in life than life itself. He kept thinking about all that had happened to him and on reaching the hotel, he settled in a comfortable chair and had a hot cup of coffee. He removed his blood stained clothes and found a sheet of paper inside his pocket. It read,

Dear Friend

I hope you are alive to read this. By this time you must have realized that I am not an old lunatic roaming mindlessly in the forest. You need not worry about me, I have plans for myself like the way I had for you. It was unfortunate that I missed out on saving one more life but destiny has its own way of running the show.

Initially, I was put into a cell which was next to yours and I could hear all that you were saying. I had mentally pictured your life, your attitude and your past from your talk. You are a hard nut to crack out of fear and worry, but God has given you an opportunity to introspect.

I want to give you an example with which you can relate. You must know about Gandhi and his fight for freedom. What will you think if I say that you too can be like Gandhi?

When Gandhi was denied his seat in the train at South Africa, he could have convinced himself not to create a scene and finish the rest of the journey standing. He could have avoided a situation and continued to live his life as always. He could also sue the authorities for denying his reserved seat in the train. By doing this, he would have still been in his comfort zone. But as you know, this did not happen. This event turned out to be the starting point for a big revolution. You were put in a difficult situation during which you must have taken a call than to expect somebody else's mercy. But by not doing anything, you are literally killing a potential Gandhi in you. Next time, whenever you try to avoid a tough decision, you must realize this.

When I saw you roaming inside the room recklessly, I thought you were like a wild animal within a cage. It is common to pity a wild animal inside a cage, however my theory is different. I believe that the zoo is the ultimate safe haven for the animals. They get food on time and their medical needs are taken care of. What if I say they that like it better there than out in the real wild? The reason is that they have lost their original character and they have been tamed to be a coward by the comforts provided. The same is the problem with you. You have lost your real self by the extra comforts which you have provided for yourself and your family and you dread getting out of it. You can find your real individuality and passion only when you come out of this comfort zone.

Do the right things at the right time and do only your things. Life's successes do not depend on how fast you run but in which direction you run. Interestingly the secret of success is helping everyone around you to get what they want in life and the secret of failure is just pleasing them all the time. Start creating your own life than competing with someone else's!

It's your second chance at life, live it. I shall meet you soon.

THE OLD LUNATIC

The Storyteller

Sankaran was standing outside the old age home, looking at the people coming and going in and out of it. He was unable to make up his mind whether to enter it or not. He went to a tea stall nearby and ordered a tea and a biscuit. He opened his little purse and took out the hundred rupee note which he had allotted for the day. Before picking up his tea he took out a pen and wrote down the expense of Rs. 10 for his breakfast. He normally skipped breakfast and made up for it with a hearty brunch at a roadside shop. Sankaran wondered how he could sustain himself for the rest of his life with this sort of money. Most of his savings had disappeared for his wife's treatment which went in vain, with her painful death. Whatever little pension he received was taken by the bank for his personal loan EMI. Sipping his tea, he went into his habit of thinking about future. He was not sure if getting into an old age home was the right option for him but he also knew that he was left with no other choice. He anticipated that he would not be able to pay his rent and the bills for long. His inability to cook or work again made him a pitiable figure in the neighborhood. After relishing his biscuit and tea for a long time, he made up his mind to enter the gate and admit himself into the old age home as an orphan with no money. On entering the gate, Sankaran witnessed a group of old people sitting under a neem tree, smiling at him. Without acknowledging them, Sankaran walked to the office. On reaching the office, he saw a young man, seated, reading the newspaper.

"Hello Sir, I want to meet the manager here," asked Sankaran.

"Yes, tell me," answered the young man.

"I wanted to know the details of enrollment in the old age home," Sankaran said.

"Do you have anybody to accompany you?" the manager asked.

"I used to have someone for me but I am all alone now."

"No problem. Please have a look at this and tell me which facility you would need," the manager said as he handed over an application form to Sankaran which had the detailed cost structure for the boarding and lodging facility.

Sankaran slowly glanced through the cost structure and was shocked to find it very expensive. He was anticipating a free stay at that place but the cost came as a big deterrent. He realized that if he had to go for an Air Conditioned accommodation with non-vegetarian food, his savings would not last beyond a year. After a lot of thought, he decided to go for a dormitory stay with the basic food option. This way he thought he will be able to get through at least for six years in this facility. Sankaran told the manager his choice, who accepted it with an annoyed expression as that option would not fetch them much profit. Sankaran was asked to come the next day with limited luggage for admission. Sankaran paid the advance and came out of the office with disappointment. While coming out, he looked at the old people under the neem tree. They were discussing politics. Some of them were reading an old newspaper and some were simply sitting there looking at the roadside traffic. One old man wore a torn t-shirt, and smiled at Sankaran. He reciprocated.

After a long trip back, Sankaran entered his house and sat on his old chair which was his closest company for the last two years. He looked at the tables, almirah and all those things which he had to forego for the rest of his life. He decided to treat himself for one last time and bought himself a packet of Biriyani for lunch. He placed his wife's photograph next to him and started to eat his Biriyani slowly, relishing every bit of it. He decided to leave the house with minimum luggage and leave the rest for the house owner. He made sure he took all the photos, gifts and the music player with him which was his source of distraction from his lonely life. That night, after packing, he went for a walk. He met his old friends and told them that he had decided to go to his son's place and was vacating his house. They asked about his health and came forward to provide monetary support if he needed. He refused the support with a smile.

Sankaran walked into the small park and sat at his favorite spot facing the children's playground. He realized that he was about to miss all this happiness in his life. He was about to bid goodbye to his 35 year history with that place. Almost everyone in town knew him as a sincere post man delivering mails and smiles without any delay. As the darkness descended, Sankaran's heart started to feel heavy. He hesitatingly stood up and walked towards his house. After reaching his house, he ate the remaining Biriyani. He did not go to bed but kept sitting on the chair which used to be his wife's favorite. His mind kept telling him that his life was coming to an end and there was no reason for him to feel nostalgic about anything. However, his heart remained heavy all throughout the night.

The next morning, Sankaran took his luggage, locked the door for one last time. He handed over the key to the house owner. 35 years in the same house had made the house owner a brother to Sankaran. The house owner pushed in a little roll of money into Sankaran's hands. When Sankaran refused to take it, the house owner said with a smile, "It is your money, Sankaran. It is the deposit you paid me 35 years ago. Given my condition, I could add only a little interest to your deposit. So please accept it for my sake!"

Sankaran had no other choice but to accept it. He felt little joy as he put the money into his purse. Sankaran thanked the house owner and left to the old age home. Normally, he used the crowded public bus for travel as he could save money with it. But today, he decided to catch a taxi. When he pulled up a taxi and asked for the tariff, he was taken aback by the amount demanded for the trip. He tried to bargain, but could not make up his mind for the final price. Sankaran went back to his old option of the crowded bus but this time with some extra luggage. After a tough ride with the luggage, Sankaran finally reached his destination. He got down, tired, and slowly walked towards the old age home. Reaching the gate, he stopped for a second and decided to go for his tea and biscuit breakfast as he was not sure of the meal timings at the old age home. While drinking tea, Sankaran watched a crowd gathering outside the old age home. He asked the tea shop owner about the crowd.

"This is common scene here, Sir. This is a place for the old ones, somebody or the other keeps dying all the time!" he said, continuing to prepare tea.

Sankaran felt a sinking feeling in his heart. He realized that his end could be similar to this someday. The thought of death never struck him until this day. Finishing his tea, he tried to get his mind back. He picked up his luggage and slowly moved towards the gate. On entering the gate, Sankaran saw the dead body of an old person kept outside the office surrounded by people from the home. Sankaran had to go to the office to inform them of his arrival and to get his payment receipt. He slowly passed through the crowd until he stood next to the dead body. Sankaran recognized him to be the same old person who smiled at him yesterday, wearing a torn T-shirt. Without a thought, he crossed the dead body to find his way into the office.

❁❁❁

It was 11:00 AM when Sankaran was shown his bed in the dormitory. It was in the centre of a small dormitory which was crowded with 15 beds already. Sankaran found old people lying in their respective beds, fully awake, while a few were on their cell phones speaking to their loved ones. Nobody bothered to speak to Sankaran but just kept staring at him as if some new creature had taken the place of the dead man's bed. Sankaran did not know what to do next and slowly began to unpack. While he was unpacking, an old man came to him and asked if he had brought sweets with him. Sankaran replied with a gentle no and continued unpacking. He took out the newspaper he had bought that day at the tea shop and started to read it. Another old man came to him and asked if he could share the newspaper once he finished reading it. Sankaran obliged and continued to read. After reading it, he gave him the paper. In an hour's time, Sankaran could see that his newspaper was circulating all over the dormitory in the form of single sheets. Sankaran started to get a feel of what is about to come for him at the dormitory.

The dormitory was way too congested and there was a small hall attached to it which housed a television and a music system. Both the television and the music system were not in working condition for over a year and the office had not even bothered to get it repaired. Half the ceiling fans were not working in the dormitory and there was no provision to keep mosquitoes away. Sankaran wondered how he would be able to pass his days in the dormitory when a bell rang signaling lunch.

Everyone got up and lined up outside the dormitory for lunch. Sankaran fell in line to get his first meal at his new home. The menu was simple. It had two pieces of roti with little dhal and a small bowl of white rice with diluted curd. Sankaran got his share and sat under the neem tree to eat. He saw that everyone was too busy eating and paid little attention to anything else around. Almost everyone ate their lunch in no time. They washed their plates and went back to bed, trying to catch a quick afternoon nap. Sankaran was slow eater and kept gazing at all things like a curious kid. He saw men carrying loaded plates of lunch to the independent Air Conditioned section of the old age home. One of the guys saw Sankaran looking at them. He came close to Sankaran and gave him a sweet and told him that if he wanted to have sweet every day then he would arrange it for a tip. Sankaran smiled without a reply. Sankaran gave the sweet to the old man beside him. That old man swallowed the sweet without even bothering to thank Sankaran. The first day was very long. Sankaran was worried but he knew that he had no second choice as he had already spent a lot of money as one year advance in the office.

The night was the worst for Sankaran as he was not able to get any sleep with the mosquitoes, slow running fans and repeated power cuts. Sankaran realized the reason for people's fatigue in the dormitory. The next day turned out to be exactly the same as the previous. There was no change even in the menu. Except for a few visitors who frequented the home, most others were orphans. The only luxury Sankaran enjoyed was the tea break which he started to indulge in outside the gate. A few old men accompanied Sankaran to the tea stall. He always ended up paying for all of them. Sankaran was quiet all the time and never discussed his problems with anybody, whereas many loved to share their problems with him. He became a mute listener over time and was taken for granted by the people in the dormitory.

Sankaran slowly began to lose it all and his life began to saturate. He started thinking of the happy days with his wife. His nights got longer as he started to walk outside the dormitory till midnight. The limited music he had in his player started to bore him and he had no one to load new music into it. Sankaran looked at his old photos for a long time and began to speak to them. He started crying during his night walk and made sure nobody watched him crying. Everyone in the dormitory had their own problems and priorities to look at and they hardly suspected Sankaran's silence. For most people in the dormitory, it was the food bell and the nap after the food that mattered. But Sankaran who wanted to get away from loneliness was pulled more into it. The crowded dormitory hardly helped Sankaran to get away with his lonely feeling. With a month already passed by, Sankaran wanted to do something about it but was left with no other option.

One night, after his regular walk Sankaran walked to his bed and decided to look at his old pictures. He looked for his bag but it was not there. He was shocked and started to look for it everywhere. Sankaran panicked as the bag contained his money, his photos and the little music player. Sankaran had no choice but to wake the old man lying next to his bed and asked for his bag. He hardly bothered to answer. Sankaran realized that his bag might have been stolen and that was something he was unable to bear. The bag was his only source of happiness and even that was stolen from him. The whole night, Sankaran tried to think what could have happened to his bag. The next morning, Sankaran sat at the office gates with sleepless and tired eyes. He had to forego his breakfast. The manager came late that day to the office, much to Sankaran's dismay. When the manager reached the office, he saw Sankaran sitting, looking tired with a pitiful face.

"What happened? Why are you sitting here?" the manager asked.

"Sir, I lost my bag. It had all my money and memories," Sankaran said in a tired voice.

"You should have been careful. Don't you know things are disappearing here every day?" the manager asked without bothering to comfort Sankaran.

"Sir, can you help me find the bag? It is very important for me!" Sankaran asked.

"Let me see what I can do for you. But first leave this place and let me do my work," saying these words the manager moved inside his office and closed the door.

Sankaran kept looking at the closed doors of the office. He was very hungry and the next food bell was expected at least after four hours. Sankaran realized that he could not afford his only luxury of tea and biscuit anymore. He was dejected and he slowly walked towards the neem tree. He sat under the neem tree with an empty stomach and an empty mind. He did not have a clue about what to do next. He had never requested for help from anybody in life and today all he could do was to ask for help. Self pity grew stronger with every passing hour for Sankaran. It was then he heard the lunch bell ring. He did not want to miss it. He woke up in a hurry and rushed to the food counter. On closing towards his lunch zone, he felt giddy and he was not able to control himself. He fell down on the ground unconscious. When Sankaran woke up, he realized he was lying in bed and the manager was sitting beside him, holding a glass of water. Sankaran tried to get up, pretending to be okay.

"I am alright now. You need not worry!" Sankaran said.

The manager felt sorry for Sankaran and also for what had happened with him that night. The manager took Sankaran to his office and offered him a special lunch which Sankaran ate, with a little hesitation at first. After lunch, Sankaran offered his thanks and started to leave back to his bed.

"If you want to call anybody, please use my phone," the manager said. Sankaran stood at the doors for a while and came back towards the Manager.

"I have a son, but it is almost two years since he has spoken to me. I don't know if I should call him or not," Sankaran said.

"Please go ahead and call him. He might be expecting your call, you never know!" the manager said in an enthusiastic voice.

The manager gave Sankaran his cell phone and asked him to make the call. Sankaran dialed his son's number and waited for his son to pick up.

Hello, the voice from the other end said. Sankaran's face lit up hearing his son's voice. With a pause, he said hello in his deep voice. There was a moment of silence and the call on the other end was terminated. Sankaran stood with the phone on his ears without a word. He felt that the little glimmer of hope he had in the corner of his heart was also lost. Sankaran could do nothing but to give a fake smile to the manager and walked back to his lifeless bed again. That night, Sankaran thought a lot about the phone call he had made to his son. He wondered if his son had heard him correctly or whether the phone was cut due to a network error. Sankaran could not accept the fact that his son could be so harsh to him. He decided to wait for the next day and call his son again. He hardly slept that night and was keen to make a call to his son the next morning. The next day, Sankaran made his request in the dormitory to his neighbor to spare his cell phone for a call. The neighbour spared his mobile but wanted Sankaran to make a quick call. Sankaran accepted it and made the most awaited call of his life. The phone rang and Sankaran was eagerly waiting for his son's answer. Hello, said the voice from the other side again.

"This is me, your father speaking, Vinod!" said Sankaran quickly, to make sure that he communicated his identity in the shortest time possible. Like the last time, there was a small silence on the other side and like the previous time, the call was terminated abruptly. Sankaran knew, that this time that his son had cut the call intentionally and there was no network problem. It was the last time since Sankaran spoke to anybody that day. He spent the rest of the day in total silence. That night Sankaran did not have dinner. He lay in bed thinking of all that had happened to him. He took a piece of paper and began to write.

Dear Vinod,

I hope you are happy with your family. I am sure you are taking care of Khadija in the best possible way. I wanted to say a lot of things to you today but it looks like you are too busy to talk. So I decided to write this letter, one last time. I am sorry to say that I had forgotten the name of your daughter and I am ashamed of it. I wanted to see her and I had saved some money to buy something nice for her but unfortunately I was robbed of all that I had. I feel terrible for not doing anything for her and I always wanted to have the glimpse of the only grandchild I have.

Anyway, I don't want to bore you too much about my dreams. I want to make it short and sweet as I know that you will be too busy to read a big letter from me. I know that you have been mad at me for not accepting your love for Khadija. That time, I was not in a state to accept your love for a girl from a different religion but today I feel that all is fair in love and war. You must be surprised at this thought of mine but let me assure you that I am saying this in the best conscious state of my life. The past two years have been a great learning experience for me in all possible ways. After losing your mother, all that I was left with was the happy memories of you and her. If I am alive today, it is because of those memories but sometimes even they are not sufficient to fill the vacuum in my heart.

My solitude for the past two years has been a silent killer. With an angry son and a dead wife, all I could do was to keep cursing myself for being alive. I tried to give a shot at life by admitting myself in an old age home but even there all that I could do was to burden myself with more sad stories. I am left with no money to spare and perhaps this is also pushing me towards more emptiness in life. Today, when I look back at my life, I realize that I have been a complete loser. Everyone in their working days try to think of their happy retirement whereas I was clueless about it. I kept thinking that if you are good from the heart, the world will take care of you. But I was wrong. Today, I am in a situation which I would describe in a single word as pathetic. You will be ashamed to see my condition and accept me as your father. Maybe that is why I have decided not to meet you at all.

All this while I was thinking that it was you who made the mistake but today I realize the mistake was all mine and therefore you should forgive me for all the problems I have caused to you. I am sure you will forgive me or at least you will make that decision once you see my lifeless body. For the last couple of days I have been thinking of what is left for me in life and what responsibilities I have. The answer is Nil. The only thing that is left for me to experience is pain and suffering. Both my body and mind have reached its saturation point and all I wish is to go to hell or heaven, but before that I want to meet your mother on the way. Please don't feel sorry as death is the best option available for me.

Take Care Son.

With Love

Dada

Note: My Son's address is written at the back. If my son refuses to take my body, please bury my body near my wife's grave.

Sankaran placed the letter in his shirt pocket and looked around. All the people at the dormitory were fast asleep. He removed the pillow and took his wife's wedding sari placed under it. He kissed the sari and moved out of the dormitory with it. He walked towards the neem tree and looked for a branch to tie his wife's sari but there were no branches within his reach. He decided to climb the tree to tie the sari to hang himself. The darkness of the night made it difficult for Sankaran to climb the tree. But the sheer determination to finish his life made him try harder. Sankaran bruised himself while trying to climb the tree and with all the remaining stamina, he found himself standing on one of the low lying branches. He unfolded the sari and started to tie it around that branch. All this while, he was not even realizing that he was about to kill himself. After tying the knot it was time for Sankaran to get down and hang from the sari standing with elevation. When Sankaran started to get down, he did not realize that the sari was not pulled down from the top and a portion of it was obstructing his path. Sankaran tried to jump a small distance from the top, but his leg got struck in the sari and he slipped from the branch and fell on the ground unconscious.

When Sankaran opened his eyes, he realized he was in a hospital with a big bandage on his head. There was nobody around except for another bed with an old patient sleeping. Sankaran tried to think of all that had happened the night before and was annoyed with the turn of events. He propped himself up comfortably with his back against the wall. He was not sure if anybody would come to meet him, or how he would pay for the medication from his empty pocket. Just then, the manager of the old age home entered the room with a basket of fruits and smiled at Sankaran. The manager sat near the bed. Before Sankaran could say anything, he said, "Please don't tell or ask me anything. The past is past and all you have to do is to change your negative mindset and start living again. Get well soon and we will wait for you. Don't worry about your bills, it already been taken care of!"

Sankaran could not say anything. All he could do was to smile at the manager signifying his apology and gratitude at the same time. The manager left the room and promised to come back the next day. He had made food arrangements for Sankaran at his personal cost. Sankaran was not sure if he must be happy or not, to be alive. He lay down and fell asleep soon. The calm atmosphere with no mosquitoes and chill air made Sankaran sleep for hours together after a very long time. When he woke up, he found food placed on the table by his bed. He could not resist jumping at the food considering the last time he had food was 24 hours ago. Sankaran enjoyed the food and felt a unique sense of satisfaction after eating. Now he was in no mood to rest but like most of his recent times, he lay down on bed and began thinking about his future.

"It seems we are too old to kill ourselves!" said a voice.

Sankaran looked around to see who had spoken. The voice came from another old man, lying in the next bed. Sankaran instantly connected to the statement with a smile and asked him, "Did you try it too?"

"Well yes, but mine was a little painful. I tried sleeping tablets. It seems that I was short of them and as a result all I could achieve was a long comfortable sleep!"

"But how do you know that I tried to commit suicide?" asked Sankaran again.

"There are no secrets when you go to a Hospital or to a lawyer," replied the Old Man.

Sankaran realized that the visiting doctors or the manager might have discussed it when they came to see him. He was keen to know the reason for the attempted suicide by the old man but he did not want to offend him by asking. To break the ice, he began, "I am Sankaran and you are …"

"I am Anustup, but you can call me Anush with h being silent. This way you cannot forget my name!" joked Anustup.

"I prefer Anustup," Sankaran said with a smile and continued, "You seem to be a jolly old man! I can't imagine you killing yourself!"

"You seem to be a harmless old man. I can't imagine anybody pushing you to commit suicide," said Anustup in reply.

"If you want my reason, let me tell you first, that it's a really boring story. So it would be better if you could tell me your story first!" said Sankaran.

"Mine is a short story. I was a happy person four days ago when my only son came to see me from abroad. He was accompanied by his wife and daughter. It was the best day of my life. My son wanted to take me and my wife back with him. The next day they planned to go to the temple at the mountain. I wasn't much of a religious person and I dropped out. They started their trip to the mountains and within an hour of their departure, I received a call saying that there had been an accident and all my lovely people were crushed under a truck." Anustup could not say anymore.

Sankaran was silent. He slowly comforted Anustup and both the old men sat together, silently cursing their second life. Sankaran and Anustup began to spend their time at the hospital together and each enjoyed the other's company. Sankaran finally felt that he had found a person after his wife with whom he could share anything. He felt lighter every time he spent time with Anustup and so did Anustup. Soon, it was the final day for both Sankaran and Anustup at the hospital. The next day, the both of them were about to be discharged. They decided to take a walk around the hospital.

"So what are your plans after your discharge?" asked Anustup.

"I really have no clue. A few days ago, I was very clear in my decision to die and today I am confused," answered Sankaran.

"What is the confusion about?"

"Whether to go back and try the same thing or not," answered Sankaran.

"Believe me, I understand your situation, but you have more options than I do," commented Anustup.

"What options do I have? Are you referring to my son?" asked Sankaran.

"Why not?" asked Anustup.

Sankaran did not answer Anustup's question. He thought for a while and asked Anustup, "What are your plans?"

"Well, you know what my options are. Why don't you give me a suggestion?"

Sankaran could not reply to Anustup's question. With a concerned expression, he said, "I know your condition but the only thing I want to tell you is that you must not attempt suicide again. You are a happy person by nature and you are bound to make people around you happy!"

Anustup was puzzled by Sankaran's statement. He asked, "Then what about you?"

"Please stop comparing yourself with me. I have been a loner all my life and my death will hardly make a difference to this world. But I am sure you must have more than just a family. They all need you!" replied Sankaran.

"In that case, I need you too. You have helped me big time in healing my pain," said Anustup.

Sankaran understood that this conversation was going nowhere. He stopped walking, looked directly into Anustup's eyes and asked, "What do you want me to do, now?"

"I want the both of us to give ourselves one more chance at life."

"How do you intend to do it?" asked Sankaran.

"Well, you have to go to your son's place and I will go to your old age home," replied Anustup.

"Both options are as good as giving death a second chance," Sankaran joked.

"If you think so, let's fix our expiry dates for our new lives. If we are not happy within this timeframe, let's join hands to embrace death together," said Anustup.

Understanding that Anustup was serious this time, Sankaran asked, "Are you sure?"

"I am sure and let that be your last question. I am tired of listening to your questions!"

Sankaran smiled and said, "So the expiry date is ….."

Anustup with a stiff face said, "You tell me."

"How about after three months?"

"Now I take your question as an answer and three months is

fixed," said Anustup.

"Okay, but one final question if you would allow me?" asked Sankaran.

"Do I have a choice?"

"Why old age home for you?" Sankaran quickly completed his question.

"Because I need a challenge to make me feel alive again! With the way you have described the old age home, I think it will be an interesting place for me to live in!"

"Good, then, let's see what else life has to offer us. Let us update our life once in a while!" said Sankaran.

"Sure, let me suggest an interesting way of communication which I always follow and propagate," replied Anustup.

"Which is…?"

"Handwritten Letters. What else can be this great?"

Sankaran smiled, recalling his history with letters. "Sure!" he replied.

Both the men decided to give themselves another chance at life. Anustup assisted Sankaran monetarily to get him to his son's place. Sankaran spoke to the manager of the old age home to arrange his place for Anustup. They parted their ways. The next three months were chronicled in their letters to each other.

Dear Anustup,

It's been ages since I have taken a pen to write something other than affixing my signature. So please bear with my handwriting. I hope you are keeping the people around you happy as always despite the deep sorrow you carry within. I must say that meeting you was one of the best things that has ever happened to me. I only wish I could have been around with you for longer. Anyway, let me start the story of the new adventure in my life.

After the last talk I had with you, I was mentally prepared to make the journey to my son Vinod's house. It was a 20 hour journey by bus. Although 20 hours seems to be a long time, it passed by in a flash. For the most part of the journey, I kept remembering my past life, starting from my childhood. Somebody rightly said that when memories overcome your dreams, you are getting old. Going by that statement, I must be the oldest man in the world with only memories and no dreams. I don't think I even dream in my sleep. I kept thinking of how Vinod would receive me. I was going to meet him without any prior information and it worried me. I had never spoken to Khadija, my daughter-in-law and that bothered me, too. But among all my worries, there was one thing that gave me solace - the thought of seeing my granddaughter. My wife had spoken a lot about her when she lived with my son for a year to take care of the child. Even in those, days Vinod never spoke to me.

After a long and tiring journey, at least physically, I reached my son's place at 9:00 AM, which unfortunately was the busiest time in the house. Both Vinod and his wife were on their toes, getting ready for their respective offices. In the middle of all that, they were also getting the kid ready for her playschool. When I pressed the doorbell, the maid opened the door. She looked at me as if I was a beggar who had entered the residential quarters. When I said I was Vinod's father, she allowed me to enter. It was my grandchild who saw me first, and gave me a warm welcome with a cute smile. I felt like crying. Too much solitude made me a sentimental fool to cry for even small happiness that came my way. However, that happiness did not last long. My son entered the hall and looked at me. He stood frozen, as if he had seen a ghost, and then continued to get ready without saying a word to me. He did not bother to ask about the bandage on my head. That second, I felt as though I was in a stranger's house. If this had happened to me a few years ago, my ego would have never let me stand there for one more second. But that day, I was standing there as an old person, with an empty ego. With all the little right I had over my son, I asked him if he recognized me or not. He never said a word. His wife looked at me with least interest, too. I was not sure if I was allowed to sit. I stood there with everyone running around me. Vinod discussed something with Khadija in private before he came to me and handed over the house key. He told me to use the storeroom near the balcony and to keep the house door closed always. He then moved out of the house with everyone following him. I stood there, wondering what I should do next. I felt lonely and I thought life in the old age home was far better. At least I happened to hear some voices although sad ones there, but here, the strange silence made me restless all day. I could not stay in the house for long so I locked the house and started to roam in the park and in the streets nearby. Thanks to the money you gave me, I passed the day with two cups of tea and some biscuits from a tea shop nearby. The neighbors kept staring at me despite me smiling at them. I wonder what goes on in their minds when they look at me.

It was around 4:00 PM when the maid came home, picking up my granddaughter from her playschool. My granddaughter smiled at me again, set her cute little bag down and sat near me on the sofa. The first question she asked looking at me was what had happened to my head. Tears poured out of my eyes when I heard it. I instantly felt that there was still someone who was bothered about me. I said that I had fallen down and gotten hurt. She advised me to be careful from now onwards. She told me that her name was Dia and asked me mine. I told her my name and she was overjoyed when I also told her that I was her grandfather. She told me stories of her friend's grandparents and her school and teachers. I listened to her and kept noticing all her features, which my wife used to tell me about in her last days. Over this little conversation, Dia and I developed a special relationship. She is an intelligent kid with a big heart.

Later that evening, Vinod and Khadija returned home. They still refused to speak to me. They were involved in their own work and I was given dinner that night by the maid in the storeroom. I told myself that this would be my life at least for the next 90 days if not more. That night, I heard Vinod and Khadija quarrelling in their bedroom and I was pretty sure that I was the reason for it. I did not have the audacity to calm them down. So, I went to sleep on the floor with a blanket and a pillow.

The next morning, I woke up early and went for a walk. When I returned, I realized that Vinod and Khadija were still fighting with full vigor. I did not want to speak to them, so I went up to the balcony and stood there. After some time, Vinod came to me and told me that he did not understand why I had come to see him after all these years. He told me that he had decided to cut down the maid's services of taking Dia to school and getting her back from there. He wanted me to do it from that day on. I accepted with a simple nod and did not say a single word. In my heart, I was happy about this new responsibility and this responsibility later turned out to be the happiest responsibility in my life. I began to look forward to taking Dia to school, holding her little hands. Later, I looked forward to taking her home from school, listening to her stories of the day as we walked along. Dia started to bond with me and even introduced me to her friends and teachers.

Although my bond strengthened with Dia, it hardly made an impact on my relationship with her parents. They continued to treat me like an unwanted guest and never bothered to speak to me. Over time, I realized that Vinod and Khadija seemed too involved in their work. They hardly spent time in each other's company. Spending time with Dia was impossible with their busy routines. I felt that the both of them lived sedentary lives at their offices which was apparent from the weight they had gained. They tend to watch television till midnight and wake up late after which they began to rush. They were enslaved by a meaningless modern life. They lived on snacks in the evenings and fast-food on weekends. They hardly cared about their health and all that mattered to them was to make more money. In the name of modernity, they had lost the fundamental values and discipline. They don't know who their neighbors are. They are lonely in this apartment. The worst part is they quarrel loudly. Dia was unfortunately affected by all this and I was worried about it. I decided to teach her good things in the best possible way and the methods I chose to teach her was through stories. Every day, after coming from school, I would take her for a walk to the little park and tell her stories that I would create in my mind during the day. She loved my stories and that reflected in her habits as well.

One day, while returning from school, Dia asked me for an ice cream which I could not refuse. Later that night, Dia fell sick and had to be taken to the hospital. It was only then that Vinod and Khadija came to know that Dia's sickness was due to the ice cream she had that day. That night, Vinod woke me up after returning from the hospital. He shouted at me for being an irresponsible old man and his words showed no respect for my age. Khadija told me she was disappointed with me then and now. These were the first words she ever spoke to me. I was in deep sleep when Vinod woke me, but after hearing all these curses, I lost every bit of it and sat up in the room like an old servant who made a horrible mistake. That night, I kept wondering all that could have happened to my wife when she was taking care of the child. But there was not even a single moment when she had spoken ill of Vinod or Khadija. I kept thinking of her all night, with wet eyes. I decided to move out of the house in the morning and go to a place far away from there. I realized that an attempt to commit suicide failed to kill me the last time, but self pity would definitely kill me this time. I didn't want to die of self pity at this age. I started to pack my bag and was waiting for the sunrise.

The next morning, I woke up before everyone else did. I freshened up and got ready for the move. In the hurry to move outside, I forgot to catch a glimpse of Dia. As I opened the door silently, I felt a tug on my shirt from the back. I turned around and noticed that Dia was standing there, looking up at me with sleepy eyes. She said in her lazy morning voice, "I am sorry, Grandpa. I won't ask you for ice cream any more. Please don't be angry with me!" She did not realize that I was about to leave the house. She had just gotten up by her own and had come searching for me to apologize. I hugged her wholeheartedly and told her that I could never be angry with her, ever.

After this incident, my exit plan took a recheck and I decided to stay back for some more time just to be with Dia, till she recovered fully. At this point, I have to tell you, my life is not all that great. All the little expectations I had from my son before coming here have been trashed. I am sure I cannot survive the break of 90 days which we have given ourselves. But, if there is something which keeps me alive today, it will be Dia and her love.

With love and respect,

S.Sankaran

Dear Sankaran

I decided to wait for your letter before writing mine. I am happy that you have found a reason to live today and this is what I wanted for you. Just because your son does not accept you do not mean that everybody is against you. It is always a single frog's sound amidst hundreds of silent frogs that disturbs your sleep. Sorry to call your son a frog, I hope I am close enough to say that.

Anyway, let me start my story, which I believe can be a breather for you. When I reached the old age home, I felt that I had been here before. All that my imagination had showed me about this seemed real. This included everything from the Manager's attitude till the neem tree's shade. Since I knew that my presence was not going to invite new friends, I decided to throw a small party for all the old guys in the dormitory. I was sure that there would be some people who might not like the idea of a fresher giving a party, so I told them through the manager that the party was being sponsored by you (Sankaran) since you were back with your family. As expected everyone joined the party which had nothing but good food and lots of desserts. I introduced myself to all of them. During the party, I made a few friends including your old sweet-toothed neighbor. Everyone was happy that day. The next morning, I realized that everyone had gotten back to their shells of solitude again. Nobody bothered to mention anything about the previous night's party and acted as if it was their midnight's dream. They were stuck to their beds and read old magazines and newspapers. Like you rightly said, it was only the food bell that they were waiting for. Once the food was done, they got back to bed, busy doing nothing. Once they got tired of doing nothing they went to sleep and woke up in some time, to start waiting for the next bell.

I said to myself that I must be far from my bed for the maximum possible time. I kept walking around the place all day. I noticed there was a separate room attached to this dormitory named the recreational room. It had a vintage television without a connection and a broken music player. Everything was just like most of the guys out here. I wanted it to change. I spoke to the manager. His reply was cold and that made me hot. I spoke to the people at the dormitory to protest and ask for a new television and music player. But no one bothered to give it a thought. They told me that it was difficult for them at first but with time, they got used to it. I was adamant and went on an indefinite fast in front of the Office. The manager got wild. He kept shouting at me for the entire first day of my fast and by the end of the second day, he had no choice but to relent. On the third day, the recreation room came to life with a new flat screen television, a DVD player and a new music system. I was elated and invited all the dormitory guys to watch a movie. To my surprise, they refused my request and stuck to their beds. Without caring about others, I pulled out my classic DVD collection and played one of my all time favorites. It was an awesome experience, watching an old classic movie all by myself without any disturbance. By the end of the movie, I realized that there were two more people who sat behind me, mesmerized by the movie. They gave me shy smiles which I reciprocated, thereby welcoming them to the movie club.

The movie club got bigger everyday and by the end of the sixth day, the whole dormitory shifted to the recreational room. I have to admit that I missed watching the old beauties all by myself. But the feeling of watching it with a bunch of old guys gave me another kick. People got stuck to watching movies at night and listening to music in the day. They continued with their old reading habits but in the recreational room this time with a pleasant music at the background. The next thing I did at the old age home with my money was to subscribe to six different newspapers for the dormitory. I told them that it was the manager who had subscribed it for them. Hearing this, some of the guys here personally went to the office to thank the manager. The manager had no other choice but to smile artificially.

One day, after dinner, I intentionally played a special classic movie in which the hero dies in the end. As expected, the movie made lots of hearts heavy. I took this opportunity to speak to them. I told them about my life and what had happened to my family and why I still decided to live. I told them about the wishes I have in my life which I want to achieve before I die. I told them that unless I had a plan for my life, I had to follow the plans which others impose on me like what most of us were forced to do. I gave the example of my determination to get a new Television and Music System. If I had not forced myself to get it, I would have spent my life with the time table set by the manager here. After this talk, an old pessimistic idiot stood up and told me that I was too old to dream. I admitted that this was by far the oldest day in my life, at which he smiled; I interrupted his smile saying that this would also be my youngest day for the rest of my life. I told him that I was not sure about what he believed in, but I believed in the latter and for that reason; I would remain young forever for the rest of my life.

After my talk, I asked each one to speak about themselves and their final wishes in life. To my surprise, an old lady volunteered to speak. She spoke about her happy past and how a bad turn of events followed by her husband's death suddenly changed her life altogether. She broke down in the middle of her talk. I felt sorry for her and for most of the people in that room who somehow had a similar story line. All that these old people do is worry and all their worry is about the same thing all the time. If the same joke when repeated cannot make someone laugh more, why does the same worry make one sadder? To add fuel to their worry, they have their insecurities and fear for the future. That night seemed to be a turning point for me. Almost everyone in the dormitory came forward to speak out their past and their last wishes. Someone wanted to spend some time with his loved ones whereas someone wanted a new set of glasses to read better. Your neighbor told the gathering that his final wish was already fulfilled after he had the hearty meal at the party you sponsored. All these perspectives made me realize how vivid life's priorities are.

With two friends at the dormitory I decided to work on the final wishes of the rest. In a couple of days time, I succeeded in making some of the wishes come true like buying a new pair of spectacles, mediating a family gathering for one and arranging for a complete medical checkup for two others. I compiled a list of birthdays of all the people at the dormitory and we intend giving each a surprise gift and host a cake-cutting session on their birthdays. With the help of my gang and the fat cook at the old age home, we planned a barbecue under the neem tree every fortnight. The menu has its limits but there will be no limit to the joy of eating it under the dark sky with all friends around.

With all this, I feel a lot is changing in the dormitory. Initially, people refused to accept that life at the old age home is also life, just like the fact that life at the office is also life. With all these changes, I felt some optimism rise in most people here. You won't believe that without my intrusion, a group of people from the dormitory had succeeded in getting the slow motion fans repaired. This is the beginning of the change I wanted to see. The change can only get bigger as things have started to move from their static state. At this point, I want to tell you about an interesting thing I came across. I was watching a television program on how to control and extinguish a fire. It was explained that first of all, the fire should be found, then it must be informed, thirdly it must be restricted by reducing oxygen and fuel and finally, it must be extinguished with the proper medium based on the type of fire. I thought of comparing fire to joy but instead of extinguishing it I wanted to increase it. The thought that came to my mind was that first of all, the fire of joy must be found - it can be even a little spark. The spark must be communicated to other activities of life. Secondly, there must be more oxygen and fuel by involving more people in the joy and finally this fire must be left to spread all around without any disturbance of guilt or fear.

I believe I have started a spark of joy in my life and my duty is to add more fuel and oxygen to it. I am not sure where I can find more oxygen and fuel but all that I am sure of now is that I am not going to extinguish it by feeling insecure or guilty about it. So, dear friend, if you are sad and alone, it's high time you start a spark of joy and slowly increase it to a big flame of happiness!

With Love and Joy

Anustup

Dear Anustup,

I was so happy when I received your letter and my happiness grew more after reading it. I had no doubt that you will make a difference to the sad old age home, but making such a big difference in this little span of time is something I never imagined. I wish I was there with you to see all the changes. Anyway, I know now, where to go if my 90 days go waste. Your thought on the spark of joy was really interesting. The more I thought about it, the more meaning it gave me. I kept asking myself how I can apply it in my otherwise boring life. If there is one thing that makes me happy then it must be the time I spend with Dia and that was the spark I decided to work upon.

For most of my life, I was a loner in my own way. I try to seek company when alone and try to be alone when in company. If there was one place where I can be alone and with company, then it must be in my imagination. It was this imagination which I wanted to utilize in the form of stories to tell Dia. The best part of the day is the evening walk in the park with Dia. I tell her stories there. Dia gets immersed in my stories and keeps asking about every detail. There were times when my imagination was not able to keep pace with Dia's curiosity. Secondly, I was running out of stories to tell her. It was then that I decided to work on them before I told them to her. Every morning, after leaving Dia at school, I started to write stories for her. I tried to add more details to the stories with vivid characters. I started watching kids' channels and tried to take inspiration from the characters in it. Thanks to Dia, I started to browse the internet for special information which I can impart to Dia through my stories. The earlier few days of writing were tough for me, but once I realized that Dia liked them, it propelled me to pass these initial barriers. It felt like I was a magician with the power to mould Dia's mind with my magical tales. I started to look for all signs of interest and curiosity from her face when I told her my stories. With this, I kept improving my stories. By doing this I felt I was busy with life after a very long time.

One day, when I told Dia a magical tale, an old lady and her grandson approached me. She asked if her grandson could join Dia and listen to my story. I instantly agreed and Dia was happy to have company. My story that day lasted for more than 30 minutes. After listening to the story patiently, the old lady thanked me and said that she enjoyed the story and the way it was narrated. She informed me that she would be back with her grandson the next day to listen to my story. I smiled and welcomed her. The next day, the old lady surprised me by being present at the storytelling spot even before my arrival and to add to it, she brought some of her friends with their grandkids to listen to my story. This made me feel responsible. I had to ensure that my story would be liked not only by the toddlers but also the people accompanying them. I decided to add colour and depth to the stories during my narration. Once I started to narrate the story, everyone listening to it including me was shifted to a different world. This is one experience I love about storytelling where I can literally read my imagination like an open book and people can also see as if it is displayed on a giant screen. That day, after my story, everyone remained silent for some time to get back to reality. This was the exact moment when I realized what destiny had planned for me. I decided to be a storyteller - to be more precise, I decided to be a useful, magical and entertaining storyteller.

From that day on, people at the park started to identify me as the storyteller and more people would sit around to listen to my stories. Some parents started to take notes so that they could repeat the story to their kids at night. While writing this, I understood what you meant by spread the joy of fire. My joy of fire had just begun and it was slowly spreading all around the park. People at the apartment started to recognize me as the storyteller and they greeted me with warm smiles. At this age, I finally felt that I had gained something all by myself. But I did not stop it with that. I kept sharpening my stories every day to suit my fans. I tried to say something informative and inspirational with all my stories and this kept me a busy man for most of my active day.

One day, after completing my narration, when I was on my way back home with Dia, a young lady introduced herself to me as Chitra, a school teacher. She told me that she was working in the school in which Dia was studying, but she taught a different class. She told me that she had listened to some of my stories at the park. She wanted me to come to her school to meet her principal for a discussion. I wondered what she wanted from me and asked her the same. She told me that she had discussed me and my stories with her principal after which the principal was keen to meet me to discuss the possibility of a regular storytelling session for junior school. I was amazed by what Chitra said and I was not sure how to react to it. In one way, I was happy that I was recognized, but on the other hand, I was a bit skeptical to take this new responsibility. I told Chitra that I needed time to decide on this, for which she readily agreed. That day, I told Vinod about this, listening to which he didn't seem too happy. Although he did not stop me, he was worried about me indulging in a new job that too when I have the responsibility of taking care of Dia. After a little thought, he told me to do whatever I liked but only in my free time. This was the longest discussion I had with Vinod since I had come to this house and this made me a little lighter that day.

The next day, I met the principal while dropping Dia off at school. The principal told me what she had in mind and about the plans she had for the children at the school. She seemed to be an ambitious young lady with the aim of creating useful change in every possible way. She promised me pay for my storytelling sessions. I was happy that I was benefitted monetarily for my happiness. I took the job and from that day on I became the Story Grandpa for all the kids in school. The kids waited eagerly for my stories and even I looked forward to it every day. Over time, the kids started to like me and even shared their stories with me. I felt like a special teacher with magical powers. I started to save the daily pay I received for my stories and this money made me more confident than before.

I must tell you that I have reached a special phase in my life where I am not straining much for anything but everything comes to me itself, be it happiness, money, recognition or love. I kept wondering all that I could have missed out on if I had not survived the fall or if I had not come here. After all, like you said to me once, the purpose of life is happiness and everything else is an illusion.

With love and respect

S.Sankaran

Dear Sankaran,

Thanks to courier, nowadays, I receive your letter the very next day after you have written it. I was delighted to read all the things that have been happening to you. I kept reading it again and again that night and every time I read it, it gave me new insight. It motivated me to do something and I wanted to do it soon before I lose that motivation by the so-called practicality of life. I decided to speak to all the people in the dormitory the very next day after breakfast. Thanks to television, I could gather everybody together on the pretext of playing an all-time classic. When everybody gathered, I told them that before playing the movie, I wanted to ask everyone about something important. Although some people were annoyed by my talk, they had no choice but to listen. Once everybody became silent, I told them what I had in mind. I asked them about their unique talents and what it was that they wanted to achieve in their life with it. The crowd became silent after my question. Not even one showed interest. I knew that these people were not comfortable speaking out and that too in front of a gathering like this.

I decided that I have to get the answer in a different way and I immediately pointed out at the leanest guy of the dormitory and asked him the same question in a slightly louder voice. He was silent and conscious of everybody looking at him. I decided not to stop and asked him again in a louder voice. This time, the individual was offended. He was annoyed by my question and felt that I was insulting him. I sensed that he was angry. This time, he was not conscious of the people looking at him. He replied to me in a bold voice, saying that he was a state level athlete. He stated that he was a middle-distance runner and the only dream he had now was to run a marathon at this age. I was taken aback by his statement; I asked him why he did not try to do the same thing. He did not reply and remained silent as if he had finished his obligation of answering my question.

After this, I decided not to provoke anybody further. I asked the gathering if there was any other sportsperson in the crowd. Nobody answered. I asked if there was an engineer. Still there was no answer. I asked if there was a musician or artist in the gathering. Two hands went up; I finally got my breath back. I asked them individually about their specialties and their wishes. The first person replied that he was a guitar player at some point in life after which he had to forego this passion as it did not help him make money. The second told that he was an artist and he made a living by teaching kids to draw at a private school. Both of these people said that they did not have special dreams but given a chance, they did want to continue their passion for the love of it. After this, the oldest-looking person in the room woke up from his seat and informed the gathering that he was a lawyer and he had not been that successful in his career. He also said that he loved reading the newspaper from end to end and that he was a good writer. Then, people slowly loosened up and started discussing their passions and their past careers. Eventually, the discussion began to take shape and people started encouraging each other to pursue their wishes and passions. This discussion continued for some more time after which I felt that my voice would not be heard anymore and hence I decided to leave the rest of the talk to them. Once the talk slowed down, I played the movie and allowed the television to do the rest of the talking.

That evening, I decided to take a small ride in the city. I took the athlete, the guitarist and the artist with me. They had no clue where I was taking them. First, I visited a sports shop where I bought running shoes for the athlete. The athlete was surprised and reluctant to accept my gift. I forced him to take it. Similarly, I bought a guitar for the guitarist and a professional drawing set for the artist. They were humbled by my generosity and were not sure how to thank me. I told them that I had done this to keep myself happy. I explained that when I saw someone my age running a marathon, I would be inspired. Secondly, I loved to listen to the guitar and finally, I cherished looking at beautiful paintings. They were not convinced with my explanation but were very happy.

You must be thinking that I am buying them happiness, but believe me, I am not. It is actually them who are getting happiness for free. If somebody tells me that this was possible because of the money I had, they are wrong. The people I had bought the gifts for had wished for it badly. After their wishes, all they had to do was to ask. If it had not been me, then somebody else would have bought it for them. I am sticking to my principle that money cannot buy happiness and it can only help. My money had helped them to be happy for free and similarly their actions can make me happy for free.

The very next day, I woke the athlete up well before his usual waking time and forced him to freshen up and to wear his shoes. I took him to the ground nearby and asked him to warm up for a run. He understood what I was trying to do. He warmed up a little and started to run like a pro. He continued to run about 1000 meters after which he stopped. He came to me and said that it would not be easy now. I told him that I was confident about him provided he satisfied one golden condition. He was all ears. I told him that he must run at least one step more than his previous day. He smiled and accepted the golden condition. Similarly, I asked the guitarist to play music for everyone after dinner and at every gathering like that of the barbeque. He accepted my request with a smile. On one such occasion, when he was playing the guitar under the neem tree, some people joined him by singing along. This was an amazing experience for me as they sounded good and the respite I had by listening to it cannot be explained.

As far as the painter was concerned, I challenged him to make one painting everyday, which I knew was too big a challenge for a man of his age. However, he accepted it as he had nothing to lose. He started to draw paintings based on the themes from the people in the dormitory. After he had drawn about ten pictures, I asked him to take them along and accompany me into the city.

With some pestering and a little kick to the manager at a local art gallery, I displayed the paintings at the entrance. Seven were sold the same day for good prices. I told my old artist that I would like to keep half the money as a part of our Dormitory Fund. He pushed the entire amount into my hands and told me to take everything as he believed that he can make much more in the future for himself.

Sankaran, I am happy today because of the expectations I have for tomorrow. Friday evenings are happier than Sunday Mornings. A kid feels happier holding a chocolate than eating it and finally, buying a movie ticket gives more delight than actually watching the movie. Just like this, I am living a Friday night where everyone is happy including me, looking ahead at a great weekend. I don't mind living a Friday night everyday for the rest of my life as long as I know that the weekend is just a night away.

With Love and Joy,

Anustup

Dear Anustup,

Your letter is a delight to read and so are your thoughts on happiness. I will not accept your statement that I had motivated you by my actions. I am just a simple man living life in the simplest way possible, that too, because of you. My life here has been a roller coaster ride for the past few days. Somebody rightly said that life is something that happens to you when you are busy making other plans. The same life happened to me as well.

My new career as a storyteller is a huge success. Kids shout with joy whenever I enter the class and get totally immersed in my imaginative tales. Teachers started to frequent my storytelling sessions which made me responsible. I had taken this job seriously and thankfully, I love doing this. One day, one of the teachers asked me about the secret of my success as a storyteller. I could not answer immediately and my answer that time was passion. But later that day, when I went home and gave it deeper thought, I realized that my early profession as a post man helped me become a good storyteller. I spent a major portion of my working life as a postman in a small village where most people were illiterate. I read the letters out when I delivered them to the illiterate recipients. With time, I knew a lot about the people there, personally. I realized how important these letters were to them and what they expected out of them. I decided to do something about it and then began to develop my own way of letter-reading based on the reactions from the people's faces. I made sure that my version did not change or affect the crux of the letter, but enhanced the positive mood of the listener. Today, I use the same technique in my storytelling methods where I twist and turn my prewritten tale based on the kids' reactions. The only difference is that I have the liberty to manipulate the story in any way and still not be worried about the one which I had intended to tell.

One day, during a session, I noticed two young men sitting in the back with some kids. I assumed them to be either new recruits or parents, but they were neither. After class, these men approached me and told me that they were employees of a publishing house and they had heard about my stories through one of the teachers at the school. They also told me that they were impressed with my stories and wanted me to compile them into a book. They gave me an advance cheque even before I said yes. The only condition they had was that I should complete the book within a time span of eight months. I accepted their condition wholeheartedly as I was already penning all my stories in a rough notebook every night.

The advance amount which the men gave me startled me. It was equal to my one year salary which I received at the end of my career as a postman. The first thing I did with that money was to buy a special gift for Dia. I went to a toy store and bought her a life-sized stuffed toy - a bear. The second thing I bought her was a beautiful frock which I saw at the dress store while walking her to the school. With the rest of the money I decided to buy a gold chain for my daughter-in-law. I was not sure how she would react to it but I thought I had to do this.

That evening, Khadija came home early from office and was busy preparing dinner for the family. She was tired and it looked like work was taking a toll on her stamina. I approached her and told her that I had something to tell her. She was irritated by my intrusion and like always, she anticipated an old man's advice from me. I told her that ever since their wedding, I had never formally welcomed her in to the family and that I was also too harsh with my reactions to the wedding, initially. But after spending some time with the family I realized that the new family was possible only because of her devoted efforts right from the morning till late at night. I appreciated her for her advancement in her career as well. Finally, I gave her the gift which I held for her, wrapped in a decorated box. Khadija was taken aback by my words and my gift. Her eyes became wet and she instantly touched my feet to seek my blessings. After getting my wholehearted blessings, she told me in a broken voice that she never thought that someone would ever acknowledge her efforts for the family. She also told me that her marriage had also created a rift between her and her parents. She was afraid that she might not speak to them ever again. I realized the pain she was going through and promised her that I would speak to her parents and try to pacify them. Finally, I gave her one more surprise which I was holding with myself for a very long time. It was the secret recipe book that my wife had, which she treasured during her younger days. After presenting Khadija with this book, I told her that this book had the secret to hypnotize Vinod. Khadija smiled and promised to try out something from it every day.

That night, I decided to speak to Vinod to sort out our differences but he did not return home till late night. At midnight, Khadija received a call and her face went pale. Vinod had met with an accident while returning from office and was admitted in a hospital nearby. We rushed to hospital and found Vinod lying in the Intensive Care Unit. I could not control my emotions seeing him with bandages all over him. The doctors refused to give us any information as they felt it was too early to come to a conclusion. My heart began to beat faster and my mind went blank. With all the little control I had over myself, I reached an empty room in a corner and poured out my emotions, shouting loudly. I shouted at God and asked for help repeatedly and asked him to take my life and give it to Vinod. That day, I wished all that I could have possibly done for Vinod, ever since he was a child. I was also cursing myself for all the mistakes I had made which had troubled him. The next day, I was woken up by a smiling nurse. She told me that Vinod was out of danger and that I could go and see him. I hurried like a small kid running to see his injured father. Once I was by Vinod's side, I saw him smiling at me indicating all was well and that I need not worry. I could not say a word and sat beside him along with Khadija and Dia.

Vinod had hurt his head and both his legs in the accident. The doctors said that there was no serious damage to his head however his legs were badly fractured and that it would need at least a couple of months before which he could even think of walking. After a week's time at the hospital, Vinod was declared fit enough to be discharged and sent home in a wheel chair. At home, Vinod looked like a motionless tiger tied to a wheel chair. He felt useless and this kept him in a bad mood for most of the time. Khadija assisted him in all possible ways, starting from cleaning him to collecting his waste. This was something Vinod was not prepared to handle but he had no other choice. One day, I told Khadija to stop all that she was doing and to get back to her regular work. I volunteered to do all that she was doing. I was mentally prepared to forego my story time and to take care of my only son which was a priority. Khadija refused to oblige but I had to force her to accept my request. Vinod felt helpless lying on the bed amidst our conversations.

My life took a U-turn when my middle aged son became a baby again for me. The only exception was that he spoke more this time. I began to speak a lot with Vinod to keep up his morale, but he never took my words seriously as he believed he knew more than a village post master did. This never bothered me as I knew that he needed solace and who better to give it to him other than his father? My understanding with Vinod slowly built up with time and he even started to discuss his life with me. On one occasion I discussed my stories with him which interested him very much. One day, I decided to get him out of the four walls and take him to the school with Dia.

Once I reached school, the kids surrounded me and asked me to come back again to tell stories. I was in an embarrassing situation where I had to say no, but Vinod interrupted me and told the kids that their favorite grandpa would start telling them stories from tomorrow. I felt strange when Vinod made that statement and asked him why he had said that. Vinod told me that he was okay with me telling stories meanwhile he would spend time in the playground watching kids play cricket. I was aware of the fact that cricket interested Vinod since his childhood days and he had even played in the state level matches. However, he had to forego all of it for a career that lured him with money and stability. I thought this was the best opportunity for me to leave Vinod to boost his morale rather than sitting idle at home.

One day, after finishing my story, when I was returning to pick Vinod up, I noticed that he was chatting with the students at the grounds. He was giving them tips on the game and the students were listening to him keenly. I stood near a tree and waited for Vinod to complete his chat. Once he was done, I went to him and casually asked him what he was discussing with the students. He told me that the school cricket team was getting ready for the inter school cricket championship and that he was giving them some tips on the game. The next day, I saw that Vinod was anchored at the centre of the playing field as an umpire-cum-coach. Every day, Vinod's involvement increased with the team and so did the student's involvement with Vinod. Vinod started to love his new hobby and he started to spend more time with the students, helping them with their game.

One day, in the morning, a few students from the school came to our house and asked Vinod to help them prepare for their first match the next day. Vinod immediately went to the ground with their help. He insisted that I take rest and come to school only when he called. I accepted it for his sake; but I was restless within. I went to school to take a look at the proceedings. Vinod had made the students sit and was addressing them. I overheard his talk from behind a tree. The first thing he did was to make all the bowlers in the team jog around the ground once. He gathered all the batsmen around and told them that the first rule of thumb for good batting was to watch the ball all the time. He said that a good batsman watched the ball right from the arms of the bowler till it touched his bat. He also said that one must always make sure that the ball was hit from the centre of the bat with its full face open and not to use the cross-bat at any cost. If one did these two things properly, his body would automatically adjust itself to play every shot in the book. One must watch the placement on the field to plan his run without making a judgment mistake. This insight explained with such articulation amazed me. After discussing some more aspects of batting, he told them to jog around the ground for a warm up and called the bowlers. He told the bowlers that the first rule for a good bowler is to watch the Batsman's eye while bowling. He told them that the main objective of the bowler is to deceive the batsman by the movement of the ball so that he missed it on its approach towards him. This deception could either be in the ball's swing, spin, speed or bounce. He gave the bowlers other tips and techniques. I listened to all this and felt that my knowledge of cricket had taken a giant leap within a few minutes behind the tree.

The next day, Vinod asked me to take him to the ground early in the morning. I understood his keenness to watch the day's game and I obliged. That day, during the match, I saw Vinod in the most animated form ever. He motivated the team every time they had a setback in the game and kept changing the strategies for the team at every stage. The game was taken to the last over and the tension was high. Vinod's constant talk and techniques kept the team away from pressure and this made them win the match with three balls to spare. The team was overjoyed and they were all over Vinod, hugging him. I could see tears in Vinod's eyes and a smile on his face.

One of the stories I had told the kids was inspired from the movie named The Hulk, where the hero gets powerful whenever he gets angry. The angrier he gets, the more powerful he becomes. I believe the same concept can be applied to positivity in life. The more positive one gets, the more powerful he becomes to attract goodness in his life. I saw this happening with me and now with Vinod.

With love and respect,

S. Sankaran

Dear Sankaran,

The first thing that I must tell you is that I love the way you write your letter and also the way you sequence your thoughts. Going by this I have no doubt that your book will be a big hit, so congratulations in advance. I agree that life is unpredictable in most instances but when you look deeper, you will realize that all of it happens for a reason. Your granddaughter's keenness for your stories and your son breaking his leg has to be for a reason. If only we look at all this from that angle, we will find more solutions than problems.

My life here has become active and the old age home is not boring anymore. Everyone is busy with something or the other and all that happened because of the old lawyer in the house. One day, after breakfast, when everyone was busy in the recreational room, I noticed that the lawyer was busy cutting a newspaper. On enquiry, he told me that he loved the reader's letter section of the paper and he normally cut them out for reference. I asked him what reference he was speaking about. He told me with a smile that he loved writing petitions to the Government based on people's problems and he used this section of the newspaper as a reference in his petitions. He pointed out the latest petition he was writing, which was about the poor condition of the roads in the same locality where we lived. He told me that he had been reading many letters addressing the same problem but no action was taken so far. I asked if his petition had yielded any benefit so far. He said that the success ratio was discouraging but it did not deter him from writing the petition as he believed it was his duty to write one.

I loved the attitude of this old restless lawyer. But, I felt that he was doing a futile job. I did not want to discourage him by saying that to him, but I asked if something else could be done to rectify this problem. With a smile, he said that the only other option we had was to construct new roads by ourselves. I instantly liked the idea and asked about the cost involved for that. He was taken a back with my enquiry. That day, during lunch, I announced that I had some interesting work for everyone. When people began to show interest, I told them that we would be visiting all the houses in the locality to collect money to construct a new road. No one had a clue about what I was telling them. Later, I clearly elucidated the issue with a little help from the lawyer. Many did not like my idea of going to homes to collect money. I told them that it would be difficult to begin with but it would get easier if we persisted. I told them that the fund we intended to collect was for people from whom we were collecting money and people would trust us if we told them our intentions. Despite my explanation, only a few volunteered for the job. One of the volunteers told me that his son was a builder and that he could help in laying the road at a subsidized rate. That second, I felt things had already started to take shape.

The next day, I wrote a detailed letter about the potholed road and its problems with the help of the lawyer and made a few copies of it. I distributed it to all the volunteers and we decided to take our first step towards the fund collection by visiting houses. We divided ourselves into two teams, one led by me and the other by the lawyer. As expected, we were looked at with doubt and disgust in our first round, but a few people liked our intentions and helped us with little donations.

Our first outing for the donations did not yield good results and this did not deter us from making more trips. The reactions of people and their stories kept us motivated to continue our journey. We were slowly making progress but the money we collected was far too less compared to our final target. On one visit, we were welcomed by an old man who was pleasantly surprised by our motives. He welcomed us into his house and made us comfortable with a cup of tea. He started to speak about himself and his journey so far. He had lost his wife a few years ago and was living with his teenage son. He struggled to speak when was trying to describe his son to us. Finally, he told us that he had lost his only son in an accident in the same road for which we were collecting funds. His son had hit a pothole while riding his bike at night and fell prey to a head injury. After this sorrowful episode, he told us that he would like to make all the necessary additional contributions required by us after our final tally. He wanted to assist us in our endeavor and wanted to do it for his son. I agreed and left his house with a heavy heart.

Within a week, we started the construction plan and decided to complete work at night without interrupting traffic in the day. Finally, the night arrived and our team was supported by volunteers from the colony for the construction process. The work was tedious as we had to complete it before dawn. Since we had called only a few workers for the job to cut costs, most of us were busy assisting them. We allocated responsibilities to volunteers and all the work was interdependent. Everyone was on their heels and no one thought of sleeping. Once the packing was done, the road was tightened by a bull-dozer. After a couple of runs, we faced a newly laid road devoid of any defects. We felt that we had achieved something bigger than we anticipated. The early morning crowd cheered us on for the newly laid roads. One police inspector visited the site and keenly enquired about the new road.

The lawyer told him that the road which was hell so far was now made heaven by a bunch of old people working at night. The inspector smiled and replied that they were no longer old people but Night Angels. That was the beginning of the Night Angels journey. From that second onwards, people started referring us as Night Angels rather than the old people from the old age home.

The next day, our antics found a prime spot in a local newspaper under the title, "Night Angels delivered what the government could not!" After reading this, many people called us and visited us at the dormitory. One among the visitors was a NGO worker who came with a special request. She wanted us to help her organize a fundraising event for blind children, which was due in a week's time. She also told us that she did not want us to raise money for the event but to just help run the show. She wanted to utilize our overnight fame for her event. I accepted the invitation without even discussing it with others.

Today, people are busy in the recreational room rehearsing music, drama and even dance for the event. I love the vibrations here - it was nil some days ago. People have stopped worrying about their sad past and their doubtful futures. They have started to live like golden fish with a five second memory of the present.

With Love and Joy,

Anustup

Dear Anustup,

Finally, the world has realized that you are an angel and I am amazed with the magic you have created around you. I feel that you never think of obstacles before you venture into anything and perhaps that's your secret of success. I must say that I am also living a magic so far and literally a gold fish life, not bothered about anything else but the present. Vinod is doing better now, thanks to cricket. Although he is yet to walk, I am sure it will not be long when he starts playing cricket, himself. My relationship with Khadija has improved a lot and her parents have visited her a couple of times after my repeated coaxing. Finally my lucky charm Dia is the critic for all my stories that I have begun to put on paper.

After finishing the rough draft of my book, I showed it to Vinod and Khadija. They loved it and helped me shape the stories for a final draft. Interestingly, it did not take much time and within a week, I was holding my first book ever. It was a special feeling, especially considering my old life as a postman where I held others letters for most of my life. I showed my book to the people who had requested me to write one. They loved it and they got into business of launching it. I requested them to launch the book in the school where I was working and that the principal should release it. They had no problems with my request and accepted it gracefully.

The book launch was planned for the weekend and the school was open that day. I decided to give my book free of cost to all the children at the school. I had requested the publisher to do it on the day of the launch, at my cost. Finally, the day came and strangely enough I was nervous after a very long time. I knew I had to say something at the event and as a storyteller, everyone might expect to listen to something interesting from me. Despite trying hard, my mind remained blank and I decided to do it impromptu. Before the event, the publisher asked my opinion of who should be seated on stage. I told them that I wanted my daughter-in-law to be on the stage along with other dignitaries. This request too was granted. Khadija simply had no idea what to do when she was called on stage to be seated. She came to me and asked why she was invited and that she was not that big a person to deserve that treatment. I simply said to her that it was not necessary that only leaders deserved to be on stage, but hard working modern women too, because they were the ones who ran the family and thereby, society. She smiled and I sensed her joy at being seated amidst other equally important people. Vinod smiled at Khadija when she moved towards the stage with a humble and a puzzled walk.

The publisher informed me that all the dignitaries on stage were handed a copy of my book sometime ago so that they could get an idea of it before they were called to speak. This was apparent from all that those people said. Khadija was asked to speak and she went easy, describing all the funny things kids do today and also about creativity among kids and how books can enhance it. When everyone out there was talking about me and my book, I wondered if it was real or if I was living a dream. That was when I missed my wife. She had seen only my bad days and had helped me get past them and today when I am here, she was gone.

Finally, it was my turn to speak and I walked to the mike, unable to think. When I reached the mike, there was a huge cheer among the kids. I stood in front of the mike, looking at eager faces that were all ears for my talk. I felt that I was the oldest person and probably the weakest in that crowd. This thought became the centre point of my discussion. The first question I asked the crowd was if anybody thought that a weaker person can be more powerful than a stronger one. There was complete silence which made me assume that no one in the crowd accepted it. With a little smile I told them that I was perhaps the weakest person in the crowd but all of them were here because of me. I asked the opinion of one of the teachers in the front row. She told me that my question needed to be more specific as power could be related to health, wealth or position in society. I told her to consider power to be health for the time being and then to answer my question. She smiled and told me that a weaker person can never be physically powerful than a stronger person.

I smiled at her, thanked her and asked her to sit. The example I gave to counter the teacher's answer was about the mass destruction of lives that occurred in Europe a long time ago because of an infectious disease. Interestingly, the disease killed most of the young and strong rather than the weak and the old. It was revealed by a study that the bacteria which caused the disease had thrived on iron and multiplied more in a body with high iron level than a body with the lower iron level. As predicted by most people in the crowd, higher iron content can be found in a strong young body than a deficient weaker one. After this explanation, I asked the crowd the same question again and this time, most of them raised their hands. I wanted to tell the kids that it was okay to be weak as long as you know your specialty. One cannot and must not compare one's lives with others and each one was special in their own way.

After speaking for a little longer on this topic, I decided to end my talk with some advice. I told them that in life, there were only a few well-wishers who always feel happy when you win and sad when you lose, but there were people who wanted you to lose. As long as you are a loser, you will be liked and supported. But when you supersede them, their attitude towards you will change. I told them that as kids they might not be exposed to the harsh realities of life but they should always remember that life is not always as smooth as they believe. So they should always be fully prepared to win but they must also be ready to face defeat as well.

Nobody expected such a serious talk from a funny old storyteller but I believed I had to do it as I realized that day there were more parents and teachers present in the crowd and my talk was directed to them and I wanted them to accept their little ones the way they are and not to make them become someone else.

It was the happiest day in my life and something told me that my life was complete. There was nothing I wanted anymore. After that eventful day, I was too tired to resist sleep. I was sure that the others in the family were in the same condition, so without disturbing them for dinner, I went to my room and slept on the floor. Very soon, I was fast asleep. Suddenly, I heard some loud noise in my room and by the time I realized what was happening someone had blindfolded me and tied my hands. I felt I was in some kind of danger. I could not do anything as a strong person was holding me tight and taking me outside the house. I suspected that it could be some burglars trying to rob the house. I started to panic, wondering what could be happening to Dia, Vinod and Khadija. I was forced to walk a distance and suddenly, my hands were released and so was the strap from my eyes. When I opened my eyes, I saw a big crowd, including my family, shouting in unison, wishing me Happy Birthday. I was in the middle of a special birthday party hosted for me! My happy day just got happier with the party. I could not imagine so many people sacrificing their sleep just to make me feel special. I felt blessed to be alive.

After the party, my family thanked the crowd and bid them goodnight. We returned home and I went to my room, fully awake, this time. When I lay down, I saw Vinod entering the room in his wheel chair. Tears were brimming in his eyes when he saw me. He came close to me and held my hands. He told me that he was sorry for all that he had done to me. He wanted me to forgive him for not taking care of me when I needed it badly. He also remembered all that I had done for him when he was a child. I got emotional too, and I hugged him and made him sit near me on the floor.

I told him that he had made no mistake and that I had taken care of him because he was my child, however it need not be reciprocated since my duty towards him was unconditional. However, there was one way it could be repaid - and that was, by taking care of his children. This is the law of nature and he must not question it. I cautioned him against expecting anything from his children in the future as the same would be continued in the next generation. The final advice I gave him was to never have self pity and live life fully with confidence and hope.

With love and respect,

S.Sankaran

Dear Sankaran

I am happy for all that you have achieved in such little time! Looks like things happen only at the right time and we should never rush them. For your information, today is the 90th day of our departure from each other. As you know, it was supposed to be our date to take a decision on life. I have no doubt that you love life. I love life, too. It was funny to realize that we had decided to die for many reasons that day, but we did not find a single reason to live. But Dia became the hope of your life and this old age home's happiness became my mission.

These three months have made me realize that there is no way to happiness. Happiness is the way. This is similar to a saying - don't dance for happiness but dance with happiness! Our mind is such a faithful tool to tame. If you decide to worry, it brings out all possibilities ways of worrying that can make one restless. Similarly, if you decide to be happy, life identifies all the hidden happiness around you and helps you to get back to a happy life! This is why I believe that happiness leads to happiness and guilt or fear reduces it to misery.

I am writing this letter as I sit in the garden. It is outside the function hall where all our old angels are celebrating their success at the fundraising event. Today, there was nothing in the world that could stop them from delivering an amazing show. The more cheers they received, the more they got excited. They were just like atoms that kept radiating to the next orbit after every excitation! However, like the atom, they need to be excited always, to be in an energy-emitting zone, or else, they might lose it all and get back to the stable dead state which was their condition, 90 days ago.

Despite all this, I realize that there are definitely side effects associated with being happy: like guilt and fear. Once happiness becomes a habit, this side effect has to become nil. Sitting here today, when I try to identify the beginning of all these joys, I think it was our decision to give ourselves a last shot at life. The purpose of life in these days was only happiness and everything else was an illusion. Thanks to that decision, I am a happy man now, taking the least resistant path in all my endeavors. My spark of joy which started with the recreational room has grown into a full flame of happiness and has made an impact on the lives of these old people and also the little society around them, where it has reached its tipping point. Now the flame can only glow more and cannot recede.

I had a tough time to deal with my personal sorrows, but today, I succeeded in hiding it through the happiness of others. I've found purpose in life and that is to live as many lives as possible by helping others live their lives. I believe these angels can take care of themselves now and I have decided to move ahead and fulfill my last wishes in life, which is to go to the Himalayas. Once I do that, I might begin another new journey, looking for a new spark to brighten someone's darkness, including mine.

With Love and Joy,

Anustup

Note: I might not be able to write to you anymore but we shall meet once I am ready for it. I shall send you an invite for it. Please do come if possible.

THE HEAVEN

The hot Sunday afternoon showed no mercy on the players who were practicing for their first round at the tennis court. The tanned players kept themselves hydrated every 15 minutes with juice and a bite of candy or a banana. Amidst these seasoned players, there was Prabhakaran, a lean dark kid who was practicing his serve all by himself. He was neither bothered about the heat nor the duration of his practice. He was excited to be practicing with star players, that too with new balls. He was immune to the wound he had gotten on his knee and the uninterrupted stomach ache he suffered owing to prolonged practice. After a couple of hours of practice, he realized that most players had left for lunch. Prabhakaran stopped practice and decided to follow one of the players to the free lunch hall.

On reaching the dining hall, he was taken aback by the food on offer. Unlike other players, he was not choosy with his food. He grabbed all that his plate could handle and relished it till the last bite. He was not bothered about his loaded stomach which could hinder his evening practice. His little life had taught him to eat as much as possible as one would never know when their next meal would be. After lunch, all the players had a power nap. Prabhakaran had other ideas. He went back to the court and continued his practice.

Just before reaching the court, he saw a young lady approaching him, accompanied by a photographer. The lady named Shivi was the reporter from "Sports Life", a leading sports magazine which also happened to be his only sponsor. It was Shivi who had spotted his potential at a national level school tennis tournament. She had recommended Prabhakaran's name to the management for a sponsorship and succeeded in getting it. With the sponsorship, life took a U-turn for Prabhakaran and he never looked back.

"Hi Prabha, how is practice?" asked Shivi, waving at Prabhakaran.

"So far, so good, madam!" answered Prabha as he started to pack his racquet. He was told earlier that day that the people from the magazine would approach him for an interview. Prabhakaran felt guilty for missing his practice, but he also knew that without the magazine's support he would not have made it so far.

"So are you ready for the interview?" asked Shivi, offering a large smile to Prabha.

"I am ready, madam! Tell me, is it alright to wear the same dress for the interview? It is dirty!"

"No son, you need to change it. We would like to take a picture of you in this dress as well!" said Shivi and signaled the photographer to take a photograph.

After posing for the picture, Prabha left the training ground to his hotel room. Prabha had a refreshing hot shower in the hotel and got ready in no time for the interview. He wore the T-Shirt bearing the magazine's logo.

"So are you comfortable with your stay arrangements?" asked Shivi.

Prabha smiled and said, “Too comfortable Madam. I could not even imagine that this whole room was allotted only for me. I only wish my mother and my sister could have seen this place. They would not have believed it!”

“Glad that you liked it, Prabha. Make yourself comfortable and give me honest answers. This interview of yours will help you gain more sponsors in the future as well!” said Shivi.

“Okay Madam,” answered Prabha promptly getting serious for the interview.

“Let’s start with your Family. Tell me about them,” said Shivi.

“Madam, I was born in a little town named Avaram. I am the oldest child of my parents. I have a younger sister called Malar. My mother’s name is Kalyani. I lost my father to a road accident when I was six. My father was a mechanic and he was the source of finance and happiness for our family. His death came as a big blow to us and it took a long time for us to recover from it. After that, my mother began to sell flowers for a living. She continued to educate us, but in a government school, this time. After school, my sister and I would rush home to help our mother, in selling the flowers.”

Shivi smiled at Prabha, marveling at his innocence. She asked him the next question, “Prabha, how good were you in your studies? Tell me honestly as we know that good sportsmen seldom do well at school!”

Prabha smiled and answered, “I am an average student, Madam. I wanted to work, but my mother forced me to study. Her pressure ensured that I would never fail in my subjects. However, Malar is intelligent. She always comes first in class. I never understood when and how she finds time to study with all the work she does at home.”

“What else you do at your school apart from your classes and tennis?”

"Madam, to be frank there were only two reasons which motivated me to go to school before tennis happened. The first was to realize my parents' dream of educating me, and the second was the free midday meal at school. Free lunch at school was the biggest meal for my sister and me. I will also visit the kitchen after the meal to check if any food was available. If it was available, I would collect it in a spare tiffin box which I always carried with me. I would take it home and share it with my mother in the evening. To some extent, school has not only been a source of education but also a source of free food to our family."

Shivi continued, trying to control her emotions. "So how did tennis happen?"

"I was in the 9th Grade when a part-time sports teacher was recruited at school. He was a state level tennis player and had won accolades at national level events. After joining school, the first thing he wanted to do was to build a tennis court. The Head Master did not like the idea as he felt tennis was a niche game compared to other games like cricket or football. But the sports teacher kept insisting and finally succeeded in achieving it. Our school was the first government school in the entire surroundings to have a tennis court. The school also granted sanction to erect nets, buy four tennis racquets and a dozen tennis balls."

After a brief pause, Prabha said, "In the initial days, lots of students assembled near the tennis court to get a chance to play the game. With a single court and only four racquets to spare, all that a student gets to play is four points and that too with a partner by the side. Our sports teacher did not like this idea as he felt that this method was not helping anybody get a proper training. He decided to select students that he felt could be trained to be better players. I was among those eight students he selected. He trained us exclusively for Tennis and made us participate in school level matches. I took the game seriously and slowly got addicted to it. The only problem I faced was that I was not able to help my mother in the evenings as most training sessions were after the regular classes. My sports teacher was impressed by my game. I began to participate in the singles event whereas my other friends were selected for the doubles team on a rotation basis. I had a good start at all the tournaments. I could never make it to the semis even once. It was only during my 11th Grade that I started getting podium finishes. My sports teacher and my school supported me in my endeavor and provided me with money for nutritious food. That money was my first contribution to my family."

Prabha stopped speaking for a while as he felt his emotions began to overpower him. He drank a glass of water and then continued, "My game began to improve everyday as my training started to get longer. The biggest moment came when I was selected to represent my district in the state level tournament. My sports teacher began to dedicate his time in training me for this event and he also presented me with a new racquet, to be used as a reserve for my games. He made arrangements to bring my mother and sister to watch my final game. Finally, I succeeded in winning the finals. It was the first time I saw my mother cry in happiness. She was proud of my accomplishment and was bold enough to encourage me to concentrate on Tennis rather than on my studies. Being the winner of this event, I was selected for the nationals where you had spotted me!"

"That's really inspiring, but tell me what was going through your mind when you were playing the nationals final?" asked Shivi.

"That was perhaps the most grueling three hours of my life! I knew I was the underdog of the event and my opponent was also the crowd's favorite. This was putting a lot of pressure on my game. I tried too hard to play my natural game and was hitting the ball harder compared to my regular shots. In one of those backhand strokes, I broke my racquet into two. At that instant, I thought my game was over as that was the best racquet I had with me. The reserve racquet I had already had a crack. When I tried to finish the remaining match with the reserve racquet, I forgot the pressure I had earlier as I was mentally prepared for a potential defeat. From that point on, I began to play the game not only with respect to the ball but also with respect to my cracked racquet. Surprisingly, I was still winning points to bring the match to the final set. On one of the serves in the final set, I realized that the crack had become too wide and that it could shatter any time. I thought I was too unlucky but I did not want to blame anybody. In the break, during the final set, the opponent's coach saw me work on my racquet with all my strength. He smiled at me and went back without saying a word. By the time we were called to resume the match, he came running to me with a bright racquet in his arms. He handed the racquet over to me and said that it was a present to him from his opponent to play my complete game. My happiness knew no bounds and I was amazed by this selfless generosity of the opponent. I smiled at him as I walked back to the court indicating my thanks. I was a bit reluctant to fight him after this gift of his but once the game resumed, I became a different person. It was the toughest match I had played and the most memorable victory of my life so far. After the match, the opponent approached me to congratulate me on my victory and to collect his racquet. But today, thanks to your company I have everything that a player can ask for. I cannot explain the difference this has made to my game and I shall be always indebted to you!"

Shivi was totally immersed in Prabha's words. For the first time in 10 years, she was proud about working for her company. She avoided asking anything on the present tournament as she felt that it could pressurize him indirectly. However she had one more question left. "What is your future dream, Prabha?"

"I am already living a dream, Madam. I want to share it with my mother and my sister. I know that if I continue to play well, I can make money, which can stop my mother from selling flowers. I can help my sister fulfill her dream of becoming a doctor. I have a big list following this Madam, but I don't want to say it all, as I believe in doing all of it as a surprise to my family. All I can say is that I have miles and miles to go before I sleep!"

It was the night before the first match. Prabha could hardly sleep. The excitement about his first ATP match made him restless. He was already playing the match in his mind, and he kept visualizing the strokes he had to play. He fell off his bed twice, trying to hit a drop shot. The more he tried to sleep, the louder his mind thought about the game. This kept continuing till 3:00 AM and he could hardly do anything about it. Slowly, he got tired of all the games in bed and surrendered to sleep. Just when Prabha was drifted off, the alarm bell rang. It was 5:30 AM and Prabha had planned a quick practice session in the morning. Prabha was annoyed at the time as he was feeling too tired to wake up, but he knew that he had to wake up as that day was not just another day.

He drained all his tiredness with a hot shower and got ready with his kit. He came out of his room and jogged to the training ground. The cold morning prevented most players from getting an early practice but Prabha was an exception. He continued his practice which he had left midway in bed. He was confident about his game and all the fear within slowly evaporated with every stroke which he made against the wall. After two hours of continuous practice, he decided to take a break. He rushed back to his room to change for breakfast. Once he reached the room, he noticed there were four missed calls in his phone. All the calls were made by his coach who was back home, owing to personal commitments. Prabha could not call back as there was no balance in his phone. He was not in a position to top up his mobile to make a call. He decided to wait till the match ended. After changing, when Prabha was about to leave the room for breakfast, he received an SMS. Instantly he felt that it should be from his coach and he was right.

The message read, "I wish I was with you to see the first big match of your life. I know that my absence will not make much of a difference to a special player like you. Show the world, what a little player from a little village can do!"

Prabha smiled seeing the message and felt supercharged. He jogged towards the dining hall for breakfast. Today for the first time in his life that free food did not make him hungry. He drank a glass of milk and swallowed two bananas. He rushed back to jog a short distance in order to warm up for the big match.

It was 9:00 AM and the players began assembling for their respective matches. Prabha joined them after a wholehearted warm up. Standing amidst the professional players was a proud moment for him. He knew that there would be some star players among them. Sharing the court with them made it special. He was not thinking too hard as his mind had already drained itself of all possible thoughts that could erupt before the game. Some of the players in the ground were surprised to see Prabha as a contestant as he looked way too young in his tight jerseys and tiny shorts.

Prabha was allotted court number three for his match. He walked to the court, practicing his shorts with an invisible ball. Once he reached the court, he saw a tall person holding a racquet walking towards the centre. Prabha felt turbulence in his stomach when he realized that the tall person was his opponent. Prabha was called to the centre of the court for the toss. He called heads and heads it was, and Prabha chose to serve first as it was one of his strengths.

A small crowd had turned out for this match, which mostly included the friends and family of Prabha's opponent. However, from Prabha's side there was only supporter who was sitting in the bench. It was Shivi.

Prabha took his racquet from the kit. He closed his eyes and thought about his father, mother and little sister. He sought his parents' blessing with his eyes closed and said to himself that this win would be for his loving father. Prabha walked to the court and took his position to serve the ball. He looked the ball and threw it up high enough, and threw himself at it for a powerful service. The ball flew like a rocket and passed into the opponent's zone in a jiffy. All that the tall opponent could do was to watch the ball and move to the other side of the court to face the next serve. The crowd was struck dumb with the pace and the placement of the serve. They knew Prabha's caliber from the first serve that he had executed. The second serve was better and ended in an ace. The third and the fourth serve too ended up in an ace thus thereby completing the first game within two minute's time.

Prabha was happy with his service and he felt happiness within after the first game which made him confident enough to face the serve. The tall opponent, on the other hand, was stunned by his failure to connect with even a single serve by Prabha. He walked to his chair and took a bite of chocolate to comfort himself after his loss in the first game.

Prabha wanted to take a sip of water as he was thirsty. He opened the water bottle and lifted to drink. He closed his eyes while drinking the water to avoid facing the morning sun directly. He suddenly felt a sense of blankness around him. He opened his eyes but he could see nothing but darkness. He collapsed on the ground, and the water poured all over him from the bottle. The crowd watched all this, as Shivi ran towards Prabha, shouting for help. The medical team was called and in no time, Prabha was admitted in hospital.

❋❋❋

Prabha opened his eyes after spending more than two hours in an unconscious state. He could not recollect what had happened to him. Suddenly, the thought of the match struck him. He jumped out of his bed and began to panic. He started to wonder what had happened to him and why he was in hospital. The fear of losing the match began to frighten him. He got out of the room, looking for help from somebody, but there was no one in that corridor. He continued to walk around, looking for help. Feeling helpless, he moved back to his room to check if anyone had entered, but it was empty. He was losing patience as he felt that he could get back to the court and continue the game. With every passing second going waste, he thought he was missing the biggest opportunity of his life. He decided to get out of the hospital. When he rushed out of his room, he saw Shivi speaking to a doctor at a corner of the corridor. Prabha ran to her with renewed hope of getting back to the match.

"Madam, what happened to the match? I want to get back to the court, it's already getting late!" said Prabha in a panicked voice. Seeing Prabha, the doctor left the place without making any further comment to Shivi.

"Listen, Prabha, I don't think you can play the match today as the doctor says that you are too weak," said Shivi.

"I am alright, Madam! It must be due to lack of sleep that I fell unconscious. I am alright now, please help me reach the court madam!" said Prabha, getting more restless with every passing second.

"Prabha, forget the match now, it's already over. You have no chance of getting back to it!" shouted Shivi, unable to pacify Prabha.

Prabha stopped speaking. His restlessness became null in no time. He could not imagine that all his dreams had shattered just like that. He did not say a word and slowly walked towards his room with a heavy heart. Shivi felt sorry for shouting at Prabha and was cursing herself for doing that. She followed Prabha and sat in a chair that was next to the bed. "Prabha, it is alright to miss a match. It is not the end of the world, believe me!"

"Okay, Madam," said Prabha in a low voice trying not to reveal his sadness.

"Please say something Prabha. I am worried," Shivi said, trying to study Prabha's state of mind.

Tears started to pour from Prabha's eyes. "Madam, you might not understand what this tournament meant for me. I had given everything for this! I would not have been worried if I lost the match after playing but losing the match for giddiness is not something I can digest!"

"Listen, Prabha, I know it is difficult for you, but what happened, happened. Now the best thing for you to do is to relax and come back strong again for the next tournament!"

"But will your company sponsor me again for the next tournament, Madam? I don't have any money to do anything of my own, Madam!"

Shivi smiled, she patted Prabha's shoulders and said, "You don't worry, my company will always be with you. You concentrate on your game!"

Hearing Shivi's comforting words, Prabha heaved a sigh of relief. He smiled at her and thanked her for all that she had done for him so far. Shivi told Prabha to relax for the day and that he would be discharged only the next day. Saying these words she began to walk towards the exit.

"But what happened to me, Madam?" asked Prabha, innocently. Shivi stood silent. She did not want to say anything and was not able to contain her tears either.

"Madam, are you alright?" asked Prabha, sensing that the reporter was not turning around. Controlling her emotions and rubbing her eyes, the reporter turned around and said, "I am alright, you better take rest and don't ask too…….." She broke down.

"What happened to me, Madam? Is there anything serious?"

The reporter said, with a broken voice said, "Listen, Prabha, the doctors here took some tests and they think there is a problem with your health. But they cannot confirm anything now as it needs some more comprehensive tests. You will be called for some tests tonight. Please co-operate with them while they do the tests."

"Okay, madam, but what is the problem they suspect?"

Standing up from the chair, the reporter rubbed her eyes and said in a shallow voice, "Tumor, they suspect Brain Tumor, Prabha."

Spending a lonely night at the hospital was a nightmare for Prabha. Till yesterday, it was tennis alone which mattered to him, but today, he was lying on a bed, thinking of life and his responsibilities that he could miss out on. Although he tried to comfort himself every now and then with positive talk, his mind kept thinking of the worst possible outcomes.

The next day started and Prabha was yet to get out of bed. He was afraid to wake up to terrible news. He remained in bed, praying to God and his father. The nurse entered the room with breakfast and asked Prabha to eat before it got cold. Food was the last thing on his mind despite not having had dinner the previous night. He got up from his bed slowly and went to the washroom. He washed his face and slowly came out of his room. He took a walk around the hospital and noticed a small temple outside. He sat there with his eyes closed and remained in this condition for more than an hour. He got up and walked back to the hospital, anticipating the results from the doctor. Before reaching the entrance, he noticed Shivi at the canteen holding a cup of coffee. He moved towards her with fear. Seeing Prabha approaching her, she ordered another coffee. Prabha sat down near her without speaking a word.

"Did you have your breakfast?" Shivi asked looking at Prabha's tired face.

"Yes, Madam, I did. Did you eat?"

"Yes, I had it just now."

There was silence. "Please have the coffee, Prabha, it is good," said Shivi.

Prabha took a sip without realizing that he had to mix sugar. Even the reporter failed to notice it. Prabha kept drinking the coffee with the least interest. The reporter seemed to have lost her words. Prabha kept noticing the reporter for a while, expecting to listen to something from her. But, she remained silent. Prabha's little hope was shattered from the worried looks of Shivi.

"How bad is it madam?" asked Prabha understanding that he can't live in a dreamland of optimism now. Shivi tried to avoid the answer. "I know it is confirmed now madam, please tell me how bad it is?" continued Prabha.

"Prabha, listen I have to speak to your mother before I can speak to you," Shivi said.

Prabha smiled a vague smile at her comment and said, "Madam, I am the one who pacifies my family from all the bad news so far. This time also it won't be different. Please tell me Madam."

The reporter slowly glanced at Prabha's pitiful eyes and said, "They confirmed your brain tumor and it looks to be lethal."

Shivi's words kept reverberating in Prabha's ears and it had already started killing him.

"So, do I have a chance to survive madam or is it the end of me?" asked Prabha with longing in his eyes.

"Listen, Prabha. They told me about some doctor named Velan who is a specialist in this area. They suggested that we should have a second opinion from him. But, at present, he is on a peace mission to some island. So let's wait for him to come and we shall go by his recommendations."

"Madam, I don't know what your hopes are. I think I must not waste anymore time. I want to go back to my family. They need me more than I need them."

"So you don't want to wait for the doctor?" asked the reporter.

"Do you know when he is coming Madam?"

"Nobody knows, Prabha, but they strongly recommend him!"

"Madam, I don't know how to thank you for all that you have done to me. But I am tired now. I keep thinking that everything will be alright once I go home and meet my family. I want to forget everything and start afresh now. I want to go home Madam, I want to see my mother and my sister."

Shivi remained silent for a while and then replied, "Okay then, go home. I shall call you once Dr. Velan comes back."

Prabha thanked Shivi again and started to walk away. Shivi kept looking at Prabha and could not imagine if it was the same kid she had interviewed a day ago. She slowly let out her tears. She could not believe that Prabha was given only two months to live. She wanted to do something to prove it wrong.

❋❋❋

It was late evening when Prabha reached home. His mother was tying flowers, listening to the music from the radio. Prabha did not call her in the way that he usually did when he entered home. He reached the hall and sat on the floor, resting his back against the wall. He continued to look at his empty house with his mother's and sisters' torn clothes hanging in the middle of the room to dry. He thought about all that he wanted to buy them after winning that tournament. He thought of all his dreams when he left town for the tournament. Now, sitting in the house, he kept cursing God for having taken everything away from him so soon.

"Prabha, is it you? When did you come? Why didn't you call me? What happened? Is everything all right?" Kalyani asked, seeing her son sitting idle in the house.

"Nothing, I am just tired."

"Tired? Did you eat anything or not?" asked Kalyani. Prabha remained silent. Kalyani became frantic. She rushed to the kitchen and looked for something to eat. She saw a half eaten biscuit packet in a box. She took it and ran back to Prabha. "Eat this first; I will make you food in no time!" She went back to the kitchen, forgetting all about the flowers and that day's business. Prabha took a biscuit from the packet and had the first bite after 24 hours of starvation. The sadness in his heart spilled out and he cried seeing his mother working in the kitchen. "How can I die, leaving her to suffer?" Prabha thought.

Kalyani made tomato rice for Prabha which can be made quickly and which was also liked by Prabha. She served it in a plate to Prabha. Prabha started eating it and this time, he could not stop himself from crying in front of his mother

"What happened? Tell me son," asked Kalyani who was shocked to see his son in tears.

"Nothing mother, I just missed you and Malar. That's all."

Kalyani did not believe what Prabha said. She kept looking at Prabha and asked again, "Did you lose the match?" Prabha remained quiet for a second and slowly shook his head. "That's alright. You are worried for such a trivial thing. If not this match you will win the next. But don't cry for this. You made me proud by winning so many already! You have a long way to go, so forget everything and eat your food!" said Kalyani. Prabha kept eating the food when Malar entered the house. Seeing his brother, she jumped on him and kissed him.

"So what did you buy for me?" asked Malar.

Prabha stopped eating, he reached for his bag and took out a colorful hair band set and gave it to her. Malar was overjoyed and gave a tight hug to her brother. Prabha smiled.

"Stop disturbing him when he is eating food," shouted Kalyani.

Malar was least bothered about her mother's shouting. She started eating from the same plate. After the food, Kalyani told Prabha to sleep as he looked exhausted. She asked Malar to help her in tying the flowers. Malar did not bother this time as well. She lay down on her brother's lap and started telling him all the stories that had happened when he was away playing tennis.

Prabha did not want to miss all this. He wanted to live for them, if not for himself. Later that night, he called Shivi and begged her for help. He told her that he wanted to meet the specialist doctor at any cost even if it meant for him to travel to the island. He said that he couldn't think of dying and leaving his family behind to struggle. Shivi asked him to give her some time and promised to call back.

The next evening, Shivi called Prabha and told him to come to her place immediately. She told him that she had arranged for an emergency visa appointment under the medical ground basis. She told him that once he got his visa, his tickets would be ready and he could go to the island and meet Dr. Velan.

"But how did you arrange for the money Madam? Did the company help?" asked Prabha with a sublime delight.

"It is the company's employees this time, Prabha. They decided to forego a part of their salary this month and they are proud of doing it. They too are proud of you, son. Looks like you will win the match this time!"

❖❖❖

Prabha was on his maiden flight and even that did not excite him. His only thought was to meet the doctor and get good news from him.

On reaching the destination, he stood in line for the visa check at the airport.

"Why are you here?" asked the checking officer.

"I am here to meet Dr. Velan," answered Prabha.

"Doctor who?"

"Dr. Velan, I was said that he has come here on a peace mission. I have some medical issues and I was directed to meet him."

"Are you serious, kid? Looks to me like your medical problems have just started!" said the officer with a sarcastic smile and admitted him into the island.

Prabha took no notice of what the officer had said and made his way out of the Airport. He was instructed to go to the Indian Embassy and ask for assistance to locate Dr. Velan. Prabha took a cab with the money Shivi gave him, and reached the embassy. He noticed that there were many people sitting there, all seeking assistance. Prabha joined them and decided to be there with them till he managed to meet somebody from the embassy. Luckily for Prabha, the embassy had arranged for food for everyone present there. After a couple of hours, an officer emerged out of the embassy office and addressed the crowd. He said, "The next flight to India will be at 3:00 PM and therefore we request all of you to pack your bags and board the bus stationed at the entrance. For those who had come after 11 AM, please give your details at the office. We shall make arrangements for your departure as soon as possible."

Prabha did not realize that all the people sitting there were trying to move out of the island whereas he was the one who was trying to move in. There was a lot of noise in the hall as people started to hurry to catch the bus. Prabha sat patiently, waiting for everyone to exit. Once everyone left, Prabha did not know what to do and he decided to enter the office to seek assistance.

"Hello Sir, I have come from India, I need some assistance," said Prabha in a low tone towards a young officer sitting in the office.

"What? You have come from India to this place?" asked the Officer in a confused tone.

"Yes sir," replied Prabha trying not to explain everything.

"But why here? Don't you know this island is at war?"

"Sir, I came here to meet Dr. Velan for an important reason," continued Prabha.

"Dr. Velan? But why?" asked the officer.

"Sir, I was diagnosed with brain tumor and his name was recommended to me for my treatment!"

Hearing this, the Officer was stunned. He did not know what to say and continued to remain silent, thinking of what to do next.

"I am sorry to hear that but you must understand that this place is at war and hundreds of people are dying every day. Dr. Velan was called to treat the wounded civilians and he must be a busy man to meet this time!"

"Sir, I understand, but this is my final option as well and I can take a gamble on my life to save my life," said Prabha trying to convey what he had in his mind.

The officer was in a catch-22 situation. But, he knew that he had to help Prabha in whatever way possible. After discussing the issue with his superior on the phone, he looked at Prabha and said, "Listen son, I can understand what is going on, but I must tell you that things are way too violent here. I can arrange your travel to the medical camp to visit Dr. Velan but before that there are things that you must know." The officer took out a checklist from his table and handed it over to Prabha. "This is the 'don't do' checklist which you must go through seriously and remember. Every point in the list can save your life and you better get it by heart!"

Prabha took the checklist and glanced at the points. The first point in it was to check out for every step while walking in this island as most of the footpaths is filled with landmines. Prabha ran through the checklists and realized that it was not easy for him. He waited patiently in the office reading the checklist repeatedly when a man entered the office and said that the Red Cross time had arrived.

The officer stood up and asked Prabha to follow him. Prabha followed the officer to find a Red Cross van situated at the embassy's entrance.

"Go with them and they will take you to the Medical Camp where Dr. Velan is present," said the officer patting on Prabha's shoulders. Prabha acknowledged the officer's words and got into the van. Inside the van there were Red Cross volunteers who had been travelling across the island to serve the injured civilians and soldiers.

Prabha sat by the window and looked outside, throughout the journey. The van moved slowly as advised by the embassy so as to spot wounded people en route. Prabha had never seen such a deserted place all his life. There were buildings, shops and markets but there were hardly any people. He wondered what had happened to this place. The van crossed the city and travelled through the outskirts. For a while, Prabha forgot his problems and kept looking at the beautiful places that the van crossed. The van stopped at a point when all the Red Cross volunteers leaned out of the window to have a glimpse outside. There were dozens of soldiers who were directing a truck towards a deep pit in a deserted land. The truck doors were opened and inside was dead bodies wrapped in blood stained bandages. The bodies were pulled from the truck and thrown into the grave.

"What is happening?" asked Prabha stunned.

"It's a mass burial of the victims of war," said one of the volunteers.

Prabha could not believe his eyes. Was something like this possible? What about the families of the victims? Why were they not here? Prabha asked himself. Looking at the stationary van, one of the soldiers shouted to them to move ahead. In order to threaten them to move faster, they fired bullets in the air. The Red Cross van began to move faster and ceased to stop anywhere till it reached its destination.

On reaching the camp, the Red Cross team pulled their medical kits and rushed out. Prabha was the last one to get out of the van. He kept looking around and it started to create a vague feeling in him already. The medical camp was a huge tent with patients lying all around, in pain. There was blood everywhere and people ran all around the camp. Since no one wore uniforms, there was no distinction between the doctors and the people in the camp. As Prabha began to walk inside the medical camp, he noticed that all the wounded civilians were looking at him. Some seemed to stare at him whereas some had emotionless and dead expressions. Prabha did not know whom to seek for help. He kept walking around much to the hindrance of the medical volunteers. Prabha was also a bit hesitant to speak about his issue to anyone as he felt his problem seemed smaller amidst these dying civilians.

Prabha walked out of the tent to get some fresh air and a fresh view after breathing in so much of the stench of injuries and seeing so much blood in such little time. He sat on a rock and kept thinking of all that was happening around him. Within a few minutes, he noticed another Red Cross van rushing to the spot. Volunteers from the van began to unload food packets from the van. Seeing the food packets, a small crowd gathered around. Alarmed by the incoming crowd, the volunteers stopped unloading and began to streamline the crowd. A queue was formed and food packets were distributed to them. Each individual, irrespective of his age and size received two biscuit packets and a bottle of water. Many people in the queue begged for extra packets to give it to their wounded loved ones but the volunteers had to turn a blind eye to them as they had more place to go and less food to give.

Prabha kept looking at all the events that were happening around them. He slowly began to understand the gravity of the situation. He felt that he had to meet Dr. Velan soon, and get back to India before it was too late. While Prabha was lost in thought, a small girl approached him and tugged at his shirt. Prabha got back to consciousness and saw a cute little girl smiling at him.

"Hey sweetheart, what do you want?" he asked. The little girl continued to smile and gave Prabha a biscuit packet.

She asked, "Why didn't you get a packet for yourself?"

"Because I am not hungry," answered Prabha.

"But you will become hungry later, so don't miss it again!" said the little girl, placing the biscuit packet on Prabha's hands.

"But don't you need it for yourself?"

"Don't worry about it. I have saved enough for me and my brother!" said the little girl with pride.

"What is your name?" asked Prabha.

“My name is Isai Chelvi, but everyone calls me Isai!” said the little girl.

“Okay, Isai, will you be my friend? “ Prabha asked.

“Sure!” said Isai and gave a firm handshake with her tiny hands.

“Where is your brother? I want to meet him as well!” Prabha said.

“He has gone to find my parents. They were taken away by the soldiers in a white van while we were asleep.”

Prabha could not speak anymore. In that instant he felt that the little girl was in trouble and he had to do something to get her to safety. He did not know how to do it as he himself was a stranger to this place.

“So where are you going?” Prabha asked eagerly.

“I am going to meet my grandpa to get two more biscuit packets!” Isai said and walked away.

Prabha was relieved when he heard her mention a grandfather. Now that there was somebody already to take care of Isai, he had no need to worry about her. Isai walked a few steps and stopped. She came back to Prabha and asked, “Will you meet my Grandpa?”

“Sure! Why not?” said Prabha and followed Isai. Isai grabbed Prabha’s hands and slowly took him inside the Medical Camp. Unlike Prabha, she was immune to the painful cries all around. She maneuvered her way amidst the wounded people and reached a corner where an Old Man with a blood stained shirt sat on a damaged bench with his eyes closed. “Grandpa, are you sleeping?” asked Isai in her cute voice.

“No dear, I was just speaking to your brother!” said the Old Man with a smile.

"You are telling stories again, aren't you?" asked Isai. This time the Old Man's reply was a mischievous smile. "This is my new friend, Grandpa!" said Isai pointing at Prabha.

"You seem to have got a big friend this time!" said the Old Man looking at Prabha. "So what is your name young man?" He asked.

"I am Prabhakaran, Sir. May I know your name?" asked Prabha. The Old Man seemed surprised by Prabha's question.

"No one asks anybody's name here, son. You must be new to this place. I am Dr. Ezhil. I am not a medical doctor but a useless doctor of philosophy," said Dr. Ezhil without a break.

"Glad to meet you, Sir. Like you predicted I don't belong here, I am from India. I came here to meet Dr. Velan."

"Oh Dr. Velan, I know him very well. He was here this morning. He took a dozen patients with him to the city hospital for operations. He is expected back only in the evening."

"That's a long time to wait!" said Prabha, disappointed. He sat on the ground, adjusting his pants. His wallet fell off his pocket with his family photograph – it was taken when his father was alive.

"Is this your family?" asked Dr. Ezhil picking the photograph from the ground.

"Yes, Sir," answered Prabha. Prabha received the photograph from Dr. Ezhil and started looking at it with a gentle smile. "It seems that you are missing your family already!" asked Dr. Ezhil noticing Prabha's longing smile.

"I do sir. It's only these memories that keep me alive," said Prabha.

"That's a ridiculous thought, kid! How can you be alive with a dead memory?" asked Dr. Ezhil.

"I don't get you, Sir."

"Well, the person in the photograph died the next second after the photograph was taken. You are a new, alive person and not the one in the photo!" said Dr. Ezhil.

"But the memories were real once. Weren't they?"

"They were. But what's the use? They hold no significance today. You can't waste your present thinking of a dead past. Memories make one happy because they cannot be changed. Only the present can be. It's normally the hopeless lonely ones who live by the past than facing the present!" said Dr. Ezhil.

Prabha did not want to argue more on this and kept silent without provoking Dr. Ezhil to say more. "So do you want to create new happy memories or do you want to live in the past?" asked Dr. Ezhil looking at Prabha.

Understanding what Dr. Ezhil meant, he said, "Better new memories."

"So let's get into action and try to help these bleeding ones with water," said Dr. Ezhil. Just when Prabha thought that Dr. Ezhil was wasting time giving him a lecture. Dr. Ezhil turned around and said, "I just doubled my capacity by adding a young volunteer to the team!"

Prabha assisted Dr. Ezhil and started to feed water to the patients. The sight of bleeding victims with pain continued to disturb Prabha. While giving water to the patients, Prabha saw a priest in his white robes entering the medical camp. Once the priest reached the centre of the camp, many patients surrounded him and began to cry. The patients stood by their knees, while the father began to pray the lord for their lives. Dr. Ezhil smiled, looking at this, and continued to do his work. Prabha could not understand his smile as he felt that it was not a wise thing to do.

"Why did you smile? I thought that it was the best thing that could happen to these people. This prayer can give hope to them!" said Prabha in a determined tone.

"I am not questioning the hope part but what amazes me is the sudden realization of God's power by these people. I don't think they must be this spiritual ever in their life but with the growing fear of life their belief in God too has increased!"

"So you do not believe in God?" asked Prabha.

"It is difficult question to answer as my interpretation of God is different from theirs."

"What do you think is their interpretation of God?"

"In my understanding, their God is created out of their fear and every time they reach an unknown territory they make their God powerful with their beliefs. Their God will continue to live as long as fear resides in them."

"I don't accept it."

Seeing Prabha annoyed, Dr. Ezhil smiled and said, "Imagine if you know that you are going to die tomorrow sharply at 10:00 AM and you don't question that thought, tell me, what importance does God hold for your today?"

Prabha thought for a while about the situation put forward by Dr. Ezhil and answered. "Maybe I will pray for my loved ones then."

Dr. Ezhil laughed out loudly and moved on without saying a word. Prabha continued to volunteer all day and had intermittent food breaks during which he relished his biscuits with Isai. The day slowly came to an end and there were no signs of Dr. Velan returning to the camp. That night, a camp fire was put up by Dr. Ezhil to escape the chillness as well as the bites of the hungry mosquitoes. Prabha was sitting with him as well.

"Why is this place at war?" asked Prabha.

"The tribes in the place wanted their land for themselves which the Government opposed. This has resulted in war. It sounds simple. But the magnitude of these people's struggle is inexplicable."

"Where is your family?" asked Prabha.

"I lost everyone to the war. In fact I have created a new family by telling Isai that I am her grandfather."

"Are you serious? Then what about Isai's family?" Prabha asked in a shocked voice.

"They should have succumbed to the White Van, I suppose," Dr. Ezhil answered calmly.

"How can you say it so easily? We are talking about people and their lives!"

"Son, the same sentence has different meanings at different phases of one's life. I think I have reached a place where life doesn't hold that much significance to me."

❋❋❋

It was the first night for Prabha at the camp and he had a deep sleep after a long time. Tiredness made him numb to the buzzing mosquitoes and the patients cry. Isai slept beside him, holding his hands. It was at around 3:00 AM when a medical van reached the camp. Three physicians and a few volunteers got off the van and were holding torch lights in their hands. On entering the camp, they started checking the wounded patients. They found some dead bodies amidst the sleeping crowd. The dead people were slowly pulled out and were placed outside the camp to prevent infection. During this inspection, a torch light was flashed on Prabha's face. Prabha tried to resist it but someone was waking him up. "Are you alright?" said a man in his white court looking at Prabha's face.

Prabha was drowsy state and could not answer anything but stare. The man did not wait for Prabha's answer and continued to flash light on other people. "He is Dr. Velan," said Dr. Ezhil who was wide awake. Prabha came to life. He started collecting his medical reports from his bag to show Dr. Velan.

"Please wait for the sun. Your reports will be invisible now," said Dr. Ezhil trying to control Prabha's excitement. Prabha decided to wait for dawn. But he was getting restless with time.

Dr. Velan and the volunteers picked up two patients from their sleep and took them into a small room which was the only solid structure in the camp. This room served as an operation theatre for the critically wounded ones. Noises started to erupt from the room as the doctors have started their first operation of the day already. Prabha slowly walked towards the room and sat down at its exit waiting for the dawn.

It was 7:00 AM the next day and Prabha had slept in front of the operation room. Lucky for him, no one had stepped out of the room. Prabha woke up abruptly realizing that it could possibly be too late. Without a pause, he rushed into the operation room only to find out that all the physicians in the room were fast asleep amidst a dead body. It seems that they failed to save the person. Prabha did not want to wake them up and he returned around to his initial place of the Operation Room's entrance. After a couple of minutes wait, he got back into deep sleep again. After an hour's time, his eyes opened up to the bright sun which shone directly on his face. Prabha looked around and found his reports missing. He did not know what to do, he got panicked. He looked for it all around and finally decided to check inside the Operation room itself. Once he entered the room, he saw that Dr. Velan reading his reports. Noticing Prabha inside the room, he asked, "Are you Prabhakaran?"

"Yes Sir!" said Prabha realizing that the moment of truth is very near.

"What were you doing so far, it's already in final stage!" said Dr. Velan in a concerned tone.

"But Sir, there must be something that I can do," said Prabha immediately excepting some hopeful words from Dr. Velan.

Dr. Velan did not say anything for a while and then held his hands on Prabha's shoulders and said, "My experience says that you must go back home immediately, be with your family and try something there."

"But Sir, I did not do anything wrong then why me?" cried Prabha unable to bear what he heard.

"I really don't know how to answer you Son. For the last week I have seen more dead people than live ones. I have been witnessing death of the little ones in my arms. I feel as if I am guilty for not saving all these people. I feel helpless and angry for not having enough to save these innocent ones. Maybe if I had seen you a week ago, I might have replied differently, but today, after seeing all that is happening around me, I think you are very lucky to have some time to live. You must leave this place soon before it gets worse!" Dr. Velan left the room. Prabha stood still, unable to believe what he had just heard. The words of the doctor kept echoing in his ears. All the hopes he carried with him were crushed in a second. He walked out of the room without any thoughts and slowly sat down on a little rock outside the camp. He felt like dying immediately and not to wait for any more time. Lots of thoughts started crushing his mind. The thought of his family kept his eyes moist all the time.

After sometime, Dr. Ezhil sat beside Prabha. He had spoken to Dr. Velan and had come to know about Prabha's condition. He did not say anything to Prabha as he felt it might annoy him. Prabha turned to Dr. Ezhil and gave him a pitiful look. Dr. Ezhil put his arms around Prabha and began to comfort him. Prabha began to cry like a little kid in the arms of Dr. Ezhil. After a while Isai saw Prabha crying and rushed towards him.

"Why are you crying?" saying these words she took a biscuit packet stored in her bag and gave it to Prabha.

Prabha immediately wiped his tears and said, "I was just trying to fool you Isai. I already had eaten the biscuits!"

"But where did you get the biscuits? The people there told me that no food will come today!" asked Isai in a surprised tone.

"Like you, I too had stored some biscuits for my sister and I had taken a packet from it!"

"That's bad. I will never do that. You never know how hungry she will be!" saying these words Isai left the place annoyed. Prabha kept looking at Isai for a long time with a little smile and she reminded him of her own sister. "I don't know what to do now." said Prabha.

"The best thing for you to do is to get back to your country."

"I have lost hope. People are dying for no fault of theirs and I am going to die soon, leaving my family behind, shattered. There is no justice in this world. There is simply no justice in this world!"

Dr. Ezhil gave a sublime smile hearing Prabha's words and said, "This is the reality Son. The world has taught us to believe in justice but nothing in life is that way."

"But why should one suffer for somebody else's mistake?"

"If this is what you think then you must understand that everyone in this world is at fault!"

Prabha did not say anything as he was too tired to give a reply. "Let me give you a little example, Son. The very first day when you got life, you prevented the chance of life for thousands of other sperms which were fighting for life. In another way, you literally killed those thousands of other sperms just to be alive."

Dr. Ezhil's words came like a slap on Prabha's face. He could not say a single point in defense to this. He continued to sit in the rock along with Dr. Ezhil when he saw a young physician running towards them.

"There is an emergency, we need volunteers!" said the physician in a hurried voice.

Both Prabha and Dr. Ezhil jumped up and followed the physician into the little operating room. Inside the room, they saw a little boy with blood all over him. His right leg was smashed and was literally hanging from his hip. "What happened?" Prabha asked in a state of shock.

"He had stepped on a landmine!" answered the physician.

"What should we do now?" Prabha asked again.

"Hold him still while we amputate his leg," said the physician cleaning the kitchen knife with bottle water.

"But why amputate? He can be an athlete tomorrow! Is it not possible to bandage it?" asked Prabha unable to see the condition of the shouting little boy.

"I am not trying to get him to the Olympics. He needs to live to see his tomorrow. So better stop questioning and hold him tight!" said the annoyed physician who was trying to minimize the little boy's pain and blood loss without any anesthesia or blood bank. The little boy continued to shout, unable to bear the pain and he was slowly getting into a state of shock. The blood loss continued to increase despite the efforts of the physician. The physician began to shout for cotton as there was no cotton in the room.

"There is some cotton roll near the bench where we slept. Please bring it fast!" shouted Dr. Ezhil holding the little kid's frantic arms.

Prabha rushed out of the room and began to look for the cotton roll. He could not find any in the location told by Dr. Ezhil. He got restless and suddenly heard the loud cries of the patients who had gathered at the entrance of the medical camp. Prabha tried to focus on searching for the cotton roll. He finally found them rolled and packed inside a towel which was looking like a pillow.

He immediately removed it and began to rush to the operating room when his sight fell on a white van moving away from the medical camp. He looked at it again and he saw people being carried in it away from the Medical Camp. He noticed Isai was inside the van near the window, waving at him with a smile.

Prabha shouted, "Stop, Stop!" He could not stand to see Isai being carried away from him. His heart began to beat faster and he started to chase the White Van with all his might. The van had no intention of stopping and was racing away at full speed. Prabha refused to stop. He continued to run faster despite his tiredness. As he neared the White Van, a soldier emerged out from the side of the window and fired a shot on Prabha. The shot landed directly on Prabha's chest and he fell down unconscious.

❁❁❁

When Prabha regained consciousness, he noticed that Dr. Velan was busy working on him. Dr. Velan and the other physician were assisting him frantically. Prabha lost his consciousness again and fell back into deep sleep state. Dr. Velan continued to work on Prabha for more than three hours with limited resources. Once he was done, he advised Dr. Ezhil to monitor him till he gets back to consciousness. It was only in the evening when Prabha slowly gained consciousness. The young physician was standing in front of him when he opened his eyes.

"Thank God, at least you survived this day!" said the physician who was yet to recover from the little kid's death in the morning. Dr. Velan entered the room and checked the vital parameters of Prabha. After finding the condition normal, he looked at Prabha with a heavy heart and said, "Thank God, I had the opportunity to save you at least once!"

Prabha lay in the bed, not knowing whether to be happy or sad for this second life.

That night, Prabha was made to sleep inside the operation theatre itself as he was yet to recover fully. Dr. Ezhil sat beside him, checking his condition once in a while. Prabha was unable to sleep and was worried about Isai and was thinking of all that could be happening to her. "She is just a child. Will they kill her?" Prabha asked, worried.

"Don't worry. Everything will be alright."

"How can I not worry? My worries only keep growing every day."

Dr. Ezhil smiled and said, "It is a strange that even in the greatest of the evils the fear of the worst continues to haunt people."

❁❁❁

The next morning everybody's sleep came to an abrupt end when a military van stopped in front of the Medical Camp with a loud noise. Few wounded bodies were taken out from the van and were thrown in front of the camp. Uniformed soldiers from the van entered the medical camp looking for the physicians and other Red Cross volunteers who were stationed. They forced all of them to enter the van in spite of their resistance. Nobody at the camp had any clue of what was happening and they remained silent out of fear. After loading all the physicians and the volunteers the van left the place in a hurry.

That was the beginning of another awful day at the camp. With no food and water, the wounded ones began to feel desperate for their lives. Some tried to move away from the camp whereas the injured ones kept shouting for help. Prabha was exhausted and couldn't listen to the cries any more. He was getting emotional seeing the condition of patients and he walked away from the camp to a distant location. He was tired and couldn't think any more. He cursed himself for being in that place, to start with. He cursed God for bringing him to that place. Dr. Ezhil joined him with a biscuit pack. They shared the biscuits and kept looking at the Medical Camp from this distant place.

"So you feel better to be detached away from the cries?" asked Dr. Ezhil. Prabha just nodded, taking the last bite of his biscuit. "This is true with Life as well. When you are in pain, you better detach away from it to feel better. This gives you a chance to have a good look at the problem than messing it with the people involved."

Prabha was not even trying to comprehend what Dr. Ezhil was saying, he was lost in his own world. During that little conversation, they saw a military van rushing to the Medical Camp. Prabha anticipated more wounded civilians and food reserves from the van, but he was wrong. Six soldiers came out of the van and entered the Medical Camp. Prabha decided to stay where he was, owing to a strange feeling he was beginning to develop within. Within a few minutes the cries inside the Medical Camp began to get louder. Prabha hid behind a huge rock and pulled Dr. Ezhil to him. The soldiers pulled out wounded civilians from the camp to an open ground and made them sit on their knees. They were forced to look down and the soldiers assembled behind them in order. The civilians were too weak to stand on their knees and their whole body was shivering with fear and fever. A firing order was given loudly by the commander and two rounds of shots were fired on the fragile civilians without a delay. All the pain and the suffering of the wounded people came to an end as they dropped dead on that hot dry cursed land.

As the killer van left the spot, Prabha kept looking at it, totally shaken. His hands were trembling and he did not know what to do. He realized that he was stuck on the Devil's Island.

"Calm down," said Dr. Ezhil putting his arms on Prabha's shoulder.

"Why are they killing these people, what have they done wrong?" asked Prabha still unable to control his shivering.

"Well, they are young with a potential to raise a family."

"What?" Prabha asked looking at Dr. Ezhil not able to understand what he had just listened.

"Did you notice any old person amidst the dead ones?" Prabha just shook his head indicating no for an answer. "That is because the old ones are infertile and will die without leaving a trace whereas these fertile ones can raise a family in the future."

"What is that they are going to achieve out of it?" asked Prabha still unable to get the main point.

"They are also killing the future of these tribes to prevent any future uprising."

"Then why don't they kill all?"

"They need to show at least some people alive to the world media to prevent any conflict with the international community."

Prabha was terrified by the hatred showed by the Government to these poor tribes. He could never have visualized a world of this nature but today he was living in it. Both Prabha and Dr. Ezhil stayed at that location for some time and then decided to walk back to the camp as they thought that the worst was already over for the day. When they passed the dead bodies lying on the ground, Dr. Ezhil said, "No matter how developed this society becomes, it will always come up with new ways of killing people to nullify its growth." Prabha walked feebly towards the Medical camp and sat with his back against the walls of the little operation room. He started to think about his mother and the way she used to feed him when he was hungry.

"I don't know why I am here!" Prabha said with tears in his eyes.

"Son, everything happens for a reason and maybe this has a reason too."

"The reason must be a rotten death and a free trip to heaven!"

Dr. Ezhil smiled and said, "It is always the warriors, diseased and the old ones who speak of heaven!"

❁❁❁

Prabha slowly became a victim of hunger and tiredness; he slept on the floor whereas Dr. Ezhil continued to sit beside him smiling in his dream. Within sometime, disturbances started to erupt around the camp again. Prabha woke up to realize that soldiers were approaching the camp. Prabha's sleep vanished and he rushed to safety however Dr. Ezhil continued to remain in the same state undisturbed. One of the soldiers saw Dr. Ezhil and hit him hard on his head.

"Go start digging the grave!" he shouted.

Dr. Ezhil was furious but decided to stay calm given the situation. He joined a dozen of wounded old men to dig the graves for his dead people. Prabha resorted to a hiding spot behind the Medical Camp and continued to watch the proceedings. He saw soldiers pulling out dead people from the truck onto the floor. While watching this horrific scene, he saw a little girl on the piles of bodies. He felt that he had seen that girl before. When he tried to look close, he saw that the girl was holding a small bag in her hand. "Oh my God! It is Isai!" he cried loudly forgetting all the fear. He ran towards her and pulled her out from the dead crowd. Isai was not dead yet. She was moaning in pain. She had been gang raped by the soldiers. Her white gown was drenched with blood. She was calling out to her brother in pain but her eyes were still closed.

"She is alive, she is alive!" shouted Prabha, trying to look everywhere for help but his voice was not loud amidst the hues and cries all around. Hearing Prabha's voice, Isai opened her eyes. Bearing all the pain, she gave Prabha her innocent smile again. "Will you give this to my brother?" she asked, raising the packet of biscuits towards Prabha.

"Yes, dear! I will give it. I will give it. I will give it!" Prabha was unable to control his emotions and cried like a child. Prabha took Isai in her arms and rushed towards the operation room. He placed her on the table and told to be still for a moment. He bandaged her wounds with the help of cotton tapes and gave her water.

Just as he was about to rush out for assistance, Isai said, "Don't cry for me, I will be alright!"

He kissed on her forehead and said, "Wait for me, I will come back soon with help and we shall go and find your brother together!"

Saying these words Prabha rushed out of the room. He looked out for Dr. Ezhil but he was missing. He shouted, "Help, Help, a little girl is dying here!" A thin soldier noticed Prabha shouting and walked towards him. "Sir, please help me sir. There is a kid dying in this room!" Prabha pleaded him, with tears. The soldier took no notice of what Prabha was saying, he gave a big blow on Prabha's face and Prabha fell down unconscious. Prabha remained unconscious for a while and when he opened his eyes, he realized that he was dragged to an open space where more people were positioned awaiting their death. Prabha was made to sit on his knees and was forced to look down with his hands over his head. The soldiers took their firing position and their commando was walking towards the soldiers to give them the order.

The commando closed in and took his position. He heard a voice coming behind him. He noticed an Old Man was running towards them holding some papers in his hand. He was screaming, "Stop, Stop!"

The commando ignored the call, turned around and gave his order. "Fire!"

The trigger was pulled and the fire was shot. Prabha crashed, adding more blood to that bloodstained island.

❖❖❖

Prabha felt a strong shock. He opened his eyes and saw Dr. Velan busy working on him. He felt the shock again but this time he could not open his eyes. But this time strangely without opening his eyes Prabha saw everything around him. He saw the doctors getting ready to give another shock and he could also see Dr. Ezhil sitting outside the operation room smiling with his eyes closed.

Prabha felt a special warmth. He had no pain or tiredness whatsoever. He felt light and he was moving like air. He was slowly pulled into a small tube of light and he experienced inexplicable joy during every second of this being. During this passage through this light, he was overflowing with joy although he failed to find the reason for it. He continued to feel the gentle warmth although there was no body with him to carry. He slowly tried to look down from the tube and saw Dr. Velan closing his body with a white cloth. He realized that he had died but it hardly mattered to him and he could feel nothing but only peace and happiness. He remembered everything that had happened to him when he was alive in the body but even those thoughts could not bring about any sorrow in him. He looked around the light and realized that he was moving through beautiful mountains, forests, waterfalls and white clouds. He knew that he could not touch them but he felt every bit of freshness from it. He felt that he had dissolved into happiness and then evaporated into thin air. He continued to move higher and could see light dots moving all around him. In spite of them being lights, he could see faces in them. All those faces were smiling at him. There was no physical body to talk to but everyone spoke with their thoughts welcoming him to heaven.

He continued to move and was moving towards a light far away from him knowing that it was waiting for him. He moved with his thoughts and there was nothing that interrupted his thoughts. He could think only one thing at a time and it gets executed instantly with that thought. He moved closer to that light and felt that that light glowed brighter with his arrival and it expressed its happiness and thanks for saving Isai's worldly life.

Prabha, without any input, knew that there were no age difference in this place and all are as equal as him or any other soul glowing there. Prabha moved again as he knew that there was someone waiting for him. He flew with a dignified grace and came towards that light. It was his father's soul. There was an exchange of love and understanding. They did not even bother to think about their bodily family which was still alive on earth as they knew that even they have to come to heaven one day. They were not able to worry about them as well because the souls are not capable of worrying without a body. The father's soul moved away with a heavenly smile indicating that there cannot be any emotional bonding between souls.

Prabha felt that there was someone smiling at him all this while, during his journey through the ray of light. When he wanted to know who it was then the face of Dr. Ezhil flashed before him. He looked down at earth where his body was being taken to a mortuary. He saw Dr. Ezhil writing something on a piece of paper.

The Letter

Dear Prabha

I am not sure if you had ever lived happily but I am sure that you are dying happily. I know that my words on life have little relevance to you now as you are already living a heavenly dream but as a principle I make it a point to write something after every eventful journey of my life.

The stage which you are living is the purest form of life where nothing can hinder your flow of joy, but a life when born on earth it undergoes various phases only to become impure. Without the body, thoughts move infinitely, but after getting a body, all the focus limits to its five senses. Through these senses, the world begins to teach various beliefs and ideologies that pollute the pure soul. Over time, the soul loses all its originality and begins to make decisions based only on the worldly theorems and its perception.

Once the body starts to feel the emotions, it starts to dictate life's decisions. Just like the way the three colors of red , blue and green creates the rest of the colour pattern with its permutation and combination, the same way the simple emotions of happiness ,sadness , fear and jealousy create a world of situations in one's life.

Fear of any kind is an illusion as death is certain and everything else will be in transition. Man's natural state is peace and happiness and literally no effort is needed to be in this state, however extra efforts are being put in to invite sadness, sorrow and all other vices into his life. The flow of a river is similar to the flow of happiness in life. If you obstruct it, it will lead to stagnation and it will become stale. In spite of all this, life still gives an opportunity to identify the reason of your living by all possible signals around you. It is your responsibility to identify it amidst all the turbulence.

Even after all the impurity the world has thrown on a man's soul, he can still understand life when he understands death. He realizes his value when he imagines a world without him and the difference it makes to the world. When he does that, he understands that no matter what, the world continues to move on before his death and after his death.

OLD MAN

THE BLUE MOON DAY

❖ Abhinav received a mail while he was busy hiring new recruits for his restaurant.

❖ Deepak and Priya were taking a video of their child's first steps when a post man knocked on the door.

❖ Vivi was returning from his first overseas trip when he found a letter at his doorstep.

❖ Sankaran was getting ready for his second book launch at an auditorium when he received a letter.

The letter said ….

Dear People,

Finally the day has arrived to invite you for a special occasion. I am sure you must be busy with your happy lives and I promise this meeting can add more happiness only. Please meet me at the below address at the prescribed date and time.

With Love

Old Man (who helped you in some way or the other)

The address took them to a school named "Purniman School for the Gifted" and was located in a remote village.

All four of them decided to take the trip to meet the man who was instrumental in giving direction to their lives.

❋❋❋

It was a tiring trip for Sankaran, especially after carrying his granddaughter Dia for most of the way. He wanted to introduce Dia to Anustup and was sure that she would like him at the first instance itself. The village was one of the driest places he had ever seen and there was not even a proper road. Amidst this struggle, the eagerness to meet Anustup kept him going. Finally he reached the village and found the school at the entrance of the village itself. There was no one at the gate to welcome Sankaran. He entered school and found a group of people having breakfast in an open space. He moved towards the gathering and decided to ask somebody for help. On reaching the breakfast area, he noticed a young man serving breakfast to all the people with a smile.

"Hello Sir, My name is Sankaran; I have come here to meet Mr. Anustup."

The young man smiled pleasantly and said, "Sir, please have your breakfast first and later we shall all assemble together for a meeting!"

Sankaran acknowledged and decided to have his breakfast. After breakfast, the gathering was requested to assemble below the banyan tree at the back of the main school building. Everyone started to walk towards the Banyan tree and in this process took a round around the school. The whole school was decorated with lights and flowers. Sankaran noticed mentally challenged students who were rehearsing dance steps with the help of their teachers and parents. One teenager with an amputated leg walking beside him told him that the school was getting ready for the Christmas Eve celebrations that night.

On reaching the spot, Sankaran noticed chairs arranged below the tree .He took his spot in the middle row and started to wait for Anustup. He noticed a beautiful structure created in the form of a moon near the banyan tree. He wondered what it could be and kept looking at it for a long time. Once everyone settled down, a middle-aged man with a beard approached the crowd. He smiled courteously at the gathering and took to the little platform erected in front of the chairs.

He addressed the crowd. "Good morning. I am Dr. Jose, the principal of this school. It is a special feeling to welcome you all here who have travelled so much to meet a special man. By this time, you have probably realized that you are all here to meet the same person although he is known differently to different people. The real name of this special person is Dr. Raj Purniman.

Dr. Raj is also special to a lot of other people including every kid studying in this school. In fact he is the man who had created this institution from the scratch. He realized the importance of a special school in this area and today people from the all over the country come here to enroll their mentally challenged children. This school possesses state of the art training facilities and also dedicated teachers who have sacrificed their comfortable careers and have resorted to this place. Let me come back again to your point of interest, which is Mr. Raj. It was only few days ago when he called me and informed me about this meeting and also about the other things that he had been doing during his absence from the school. This literally shocked me to the core and made me realize how a single soul can make such a difference to the society.

Dr. Raj was a one of the most sought after philosophy professors in this country and his classes were attended by many famous people other than the regular students. Over time, Dr. Raj had lost interest in teaching and started taking breaks during the academic sessions. Through one of his friends I came to know that he visits Himalayas every year and spends a lot of time there in meditation. After that he comes back to the college to continue with the classes. One fine, day he openly stated in his class that he was no more interested in giving lectures as he felt there were far more important things for him to do than giving lectures. That was when he had visited this village to start this institution with all the money he had. Even after establishing this institution, he never stayed regularly. It was only during the talk with him, I came to know that he helps people like you during this break.

At this point I must tell you that I was also his student and his talks had great influence on my thinking. After heading a corporate establishment for several years, I thought it was time to quit and add some meaning to my life. I decided to be a volunteer in this organization and today I am happy that I had taken that decision. This institute is self reliant in all possible ways and it is more than just a school for the mentally challenged. This whole village depended on this for their livelihood as this school has various departments which make special equipments for the mentally retarded children.

Finally, I end my talk with sad news. Dr. Raj Purniman is no more. The moon structure which you are seeing in front of you is actually his funeral spot. He had decided his death long before and no one including me was aware of his funeral, sparring a few mentally challenged children who had done his cremation. His cremation was done two days ago, at midnight without anybody's knowledge. He did not want anybody to cry for him and wanted everybody to know that his soul was still alive amidst all of us. The letter of his death and the subsequent cremation came as a shock to us as we were not able to pay the final rites. However, in his final letter to me he had mentioned that he had selected today as the day to do the final rights with all your talks.

The gathering was stunned. They could not believe that their old man was no more. There were tears and cries all around. Sankaran sat still with a heavy heart. After gaining courage he stood up and walked towards the platform and gave his talk for

Dr. Raj. He spoke about the qualities and values that he had learnt from Dr. Raj and how it had helped him overcome his miseries in life. Sankaran's talk was followed by Abhinav, who articulated all that changes that had been incorporated into his life during Dr. Raj's short stay with him.

Slowly, everyone took the stage and began to speak about Dr. Raj and the change he had brought upon their lives. Everyone's talk was an inspiration for the gathering as they had never listened to such miracle tales. After everyone's talk, Dr. Jose took the stage said, "Although Dr. Raj is no more with us, he had written a small letter for all of us. As per his last note, this letter will be read by one of the gifted child of this school. This child is the living proof of what training and dedication can do to overcome any challenges in life."

A lean kid came to the stage with the support of Dr. Jose and began to read the final letter from Dr. Raj.

Dear People,

Thank you very much, for all the love you have showered on me, by coming here. It is an amazing feeling, although I know that I won't be there to feel it with you.

The main reason I had called for this gathering was to tell you that nothing comes to an end with my death. The show will go on and you will run the show. You will be the seed of joy for the future and you will create a forest of happiness in this concrete jungle. This gathering is a gathering of happiness. Only good things must happen with my death, and I cannot expect a better end than this, where so many people from such diverse backgrounds have come to pay their final respects for me.

The greatest happiness a man can attain is by helping others without any expectations from them. When he does that, he lives more than one life. On that account, I must say that I am one of the luckiest people on earth, to have lived so many lives through each of you.

Visualize that you had never existed. You shall see that life still goes on. The only value you can add to your life is to grow joy in others life. So grow happiness inside you, and grow happiness outside you. According to me, Man is Man's God, for as long as he is alive.

You are not ordinary people. You have seen the extremities of life. Ordinary people in extraordinary situations reveal their true selves. This extraordinary situation can be natural or self-driven. The true self awakes man from worldly consciousness and makes him look deep within.

I conclude by saying that no amount of darkness can stop a single spark of light and no amount of silence can dampen a pin drop's noise. So let no force stop you from achieving victory, and when you achieve it, you realize that it is your Blue Moon Day.

With Love,

Dr. Raj Purniman

The crowd remained silent after listening to the contents of the letter being read out. They realized the reason for their presence at the spot.

Dr. Jose requested the gathering to stay back for the function that was going to follow in the evening. Everyone accepted the invitation. They decided to spend the rest of the day with the gifted children of the institution.

The day slowly progressed and the sun set, marking the onset of the evening. People took their seats in the auditorium. There was music and festivities all around. The whole village came to life that night. All the village people were within the school to be a part of this celebration. A fat Santa danced in the crowd, throwing chocolates all around at the people. Whenever he saw a kid in the crowd, he picked him up and gave him a kiss and a gift.

While dancing, Santa noticed young Dia sitting near her grandfather, Sankaran. He walked towards Dia and picked her up, and whispered in her ears, "Hi Dia! I have got a gift for you!" He took a fairytale book, beautifully wrapped, from his bag.

“But Santa, how do you know my name?” Dia asked, surprised.

Santa smiled and replied, “I am Santa and I know everything!” Saying so, Santa walked out of the auditorium and escaped into the full moon night.